Let Go

Daisuke Yosumi began his career at Sony Music in Tokyo in 1995 and was headhunted by Warner Music to lead its production department in 2004. During these corporate years, he practised the art of 'letting go', requesting demotions twice to protect his true self. Each time, a breakthrough followed. He went on to produce over ten million-selling hits and became a J-POP hitmaker.

In 2010, he let go of his career, status, connections, possessions and 90 per cent of his income and moved to a lakeside forest in New Zealand. There, he's achieved his dream of freedom and independence – a self-sufficient, off-grid, minimalist life with his family. Since then, he has published over ten books, including several bestsellers.

A pioneer of Japan's minimalist, digital nomad, organic and trekking movements, he is the first Japanese ambassador for both Greenpeace Japan and Fairtrade Japan. Since 2016, he has led LifestyleDesign.Camp, an online community school for post-capitalist living.

daisukeyosumi.com

Let Go

50 Lessons from Japanese Minimalism to Set You Free

•

Daisuke Yosumi

ALLEN & UNWIN

Originally published in Japanese as 自由であり続けるために20代で捨てるべき50のこと [Jyuu de Ari Tsukeru tame ni 20-dai de Suteru Subeki 50 no Koto] in 2012 by Sanctuary Books.

First published in hardback in Great Britain in 2026 by Allen & Unwin, an imprint of Atlantic Books Ltd.

Copyright © Daisuke Yosumi, 2026

Translation copyright © Daisuke Yosumi, 2026

The moral right of Daisuke Yosumi to be identified as the author and translator of this work has been asserted by him in accordance with the Copyright, Designs and Patents Act of 1988.

All rights reserved. No part of this publication may be reproduced, stored in a retrieval system, or transmitted in any form or by any means, electronic, mechanical, photocopying, recording, or otherwise, without the prior permission of both the copyright owner and the above publisher of this book.

No part of this book may be used in any manner in the learning, training or development of generative artificial intelligence technologies (including but not limited to machine learning models and large language models (LLMs)), whether by data scraping, data mining or use in any way to create or form a part of data sets or in any other way.

Every effort has been made to trace or contact all copyright holders. The publishers will be pleased to make good any omissions or rectify any mistakes brought to their attention at the earliest opportunity.

10 9 8 7 6 5 4 3 2 1

A CIP catalogue record for this book is available from the British Library.

Hardback ISBN: 978 1 80546 561 4
Trade Paperback ISBN: 978 1 80546 663 5
E-book ISBN: 978 1 80546 562 1

Printed and bound by CPI (UK) Ltd, Croydon CR0 4YY

Allen & Unwin
An imprint of Atlantic Books Ltd
Ormond House
26–27 Boswell Street
London
WC1N 3JZ

www.atlantic-books.co.uk

Product safety EU representative: Authorised Rep Compliance Ltd., Ground Floor, 71 Lower Baggot Street, Dublin, D02 P593, Ireland. www.arccompliance.com

Less Is Freedom

Contents

Introduction: Why Are You Unfree Now?   1

Prologue: Never Let Go of Your Freedom   15

STEP 1: Money & Belongings   33

1. Let go of the noise in your vision   35
2. Let go of what you aren't using   39
3. Let go of the need to stock up   43
4. Let go of your stingy habits   47
5. Let go of small purchases   51
6. Let go of impulse shopping   57
7. Let go of not being choosy   61
8. Let go of accessorizing   65
9. Let go of chasing a bigger life   69
10. Let go of having too many clothes   73

STEP 2: Work   77

11. Let go of work you're not good at   79
12. Let go of the multitasking mindset   83
13. Let go of your thirst for recognition   87

14	Let go of your to-do list	91
15	Let go of majority rule	95
16	Let go of regular hours	99
17	Let go of your assumptions	103
18	Let go of your rational brain	107
19	Let go of procrastination	111
20	Let go of balance	115

STEP 3: Health & Mindset — 119

21	Let go of late nights	121
22	Let go of poor sleep	125
23	Let go of overeating	129
24	Let go of your everyday routine	133
25	Let go of the presence of others	137
26	Let go of other people's common sense	143
27	Let go of disturbing words	147
28	Let go of relying on sheer willpower	151
29	Let go of studying without a why	155
30	Let go of the noise	161

STEP 4: Relationships — 165

31	Let go of your network	167
32	Let go of familiarity	171
33	Let go of the usual holidays	173

CONTENTS

34 Let go of hiding your true self — 177
35 Let go of pleasing everyone — 181
36 Let go of resisting tradition — 185
37 Let go of checking messages — 189
38 Let go of being competitive — 193
39 Let go of hiding behind 'sorry' — 197
40 Let go of holding yourself back — 201

STEP 5: Lifestyle — **205**

41 Let go of the fear of lacking — 207
42 Let go of staying in one place — 211
43 Let go of trying to choose everything — 215
44 Let go of the fear of being foolish — 219
45 Let go of always being online — 223
46 Let go of the idea that you must never run away — 227
47 Let go of company loyalty — 231
48 Let go of giving up — 235
49 Let go of the illusion of freedom — 239
50 Let go of past success — 243

Epilogue — 249
Afterword: Humanity's Journey to Freedom – Seven Steps of Letting Go — 257

Too much, too fast, too complicated, too connected and too busy.

We live in an age of unprecedented abundance – of information, goods and choices.

We have gained almost everything – and lost what matters most.

Now, the foundations of our society are crumbling and what we once believed no longer works.

How are we to live through this age?

Introduction

Why Are You Unfree Now?

●

When did you begin accepting an unfree life?

You came into this world to live free. By nature, everyone is born free. Most of us lived this way as children, expressing ourselves freely and living as we are. Then adulthood arrives. Many people think, 'Life isn't that simple. Adults carry too much to live freely. It's time to face reality!'

But is that 'reality' real, or simply unquestioned belief?

Your Reality, Built upon 'Blood and Sacrifice'

The reality is that we have extraordinary convenience and material abundance, more than ever before in human history. And for the first time, many of us today are free to live by our own will.

Most of us who are living in developed countries have basic human rights and freedom of expression. We have the right to travel freely around the world and technology that makes our lives more liberated. Compared to nations still living under dictatorship or places still suffering from armed conflict, we have much more freedom. Compared to the age of feudalism or the world wars, we are incredibly free.

Yet modern life is becoming more chaotic and turbulent. Out-of-control capitalism and unstable economies. Social inequality and division. Racial and religious hatred. Climate crisis and frequent natural disasters. Terrorism and endless military conflicts. All of these exist alongside our freedom.

Beyond this, there are two things we must never forget. First, you were born through pain and blood. Your mother's labour liberated you from the safe but enclosed space of the womb – into this adventurous and open world. Second, people around the world, past and present, have fought and continue to fight and shed blood for our various freedoms.

'When you forget where you come from, you forget who you are.' This saying can be read in

INTRODUCTION

many ways. For me, it means deep gratitude for my mother who survived massive blood loss and risked her life to give me mine. It also includes my quiet gratitude for generations of Japanese ancestors before my mother. I know my freedom wasn't earned by me alone. I am being kept alive – watched over by countless generations past. In a way, they still walk with me.

Every Moment Is Life Itself – Zen Philosophy of Mortality

Furthermore, remember that you emerged from *nothingness*. You were born an innocent, completely original being, with nothing but your body and soul. In the earliest days, your soul was untouched, your true self free from any attachment. You were beautifully light and purely free – expressing yourself naturally and living just as you were. In Japan, there is a Zen phrase 本来無一物 (*Honrai mu ichimotsu*): 'Originally, we carried nothing – no possessions, no stain, no ego'. Your life begins in non-self, empty-handed and unburdened. When it ends, you return to your origin, your home – to nothingness.

In fact, when I was born, my own life was also in danger just like my mother's. Even after birth, I was physically weak and often ill, hospitalized for long periods with a serious disease. I missed half of kindergarten and was mentally fragile as well. In my early years in elementary school, I developed a nervous tic and suffered from severe blushing. That made me an easy target for bullying. 'Is life supposed to be this hard? Why was I even born?' I still remember the pain in my heart.

Through this series of experiences, the meaning of life was burned into the deepest part of me. Life is a rare gift, never promised, never certain.

How will I use this fleeting and fragile life that I was lucky to be given by my mother and ancestors? Whenever I felt lost or faced hardship, I returned to this question: 'How do I use this precious gift?' It became my ultimate inner compass. It helped me make wholehearted decisions and keep moving forward step by step.

We all have a limited lifespan. Time and life are finite. And because of that, time is life – never money. In other words, wasting an hour is wasting an hour of your life. You already know that the older

INTRODUCTION

you get, the faster time passes. Not just hours but weeks, months, years – all slip away quickly. Before you realize it, your time runs out, and your life comes to an end.

In the brief span in between, may you live light and unbound. Honour your time. Never waste the gift of life on trivial things. Live freely as your true self. Isn't that what your ancestors, who gave their lives for freedom, wished for you?

'Let me use this mortal life – this precious time – only for what I truly love!' The inner voice that cries out these words is none other than your soul. That is: you. Your true self.

A Strategy for Happiness in a Chaotic World

We no longer need to shed blood to gain unchained freedom. Unlike our ancestors, most of us don't face daily threats of violence from nature, animals and other humans. Yet this rapidly changing and increasingly complex world is a hard one. In an age of chaos where the future feels unclear, minimalism simplifies the path toward true freedom.

LET GO

I am not a monk or spiritual teacher. I learned the art of minimalism through three life stages: hardship in my school years, survival in the music industry and, later, life in the forest. This book passes down what I discovered. The principle is simple: ultimately, all you need to live is yourself – your body and soul, nothing more. Everything you've gained since birth – possessions, identities, habits, beliefs, even desires – has never *truly* been yours. Most were given or imposed by parents or primary caregivers. Even your personality – only half genetic – was deeply shaped by those early influences. The rest were from close relatives, friends, school, work and society. Once you become aware of this, life becomes dramatically lighter and easier. Your sense of happiness begins to rise naturally. You'll even discover you can let go of the trauma you've unconsciously carried.

To be clear, this is not a psychological or philosophical book. It's a practical guide to the mindset and techniques of modern minimalism, with real-life examples anyone can follow. I've distilled its very essence into fifty simple lessons you can begin today.

INTRODUCTION

This book is built on a trinity of core belief (minimalism), life strategy (minimalist living) and daily practice (letting go). I will keep guiding you back to minimalism's basic rules: stop seeking what you don't need, and release unnecessary burdens.

Whether by fate or misfortune, I faced death at birth and survived early childhood physically and mentally fragile. Those early experiences seem to have etched a core value of minimalism into me. Simply being alive is enough, and being healthy is already a blessing – do I need anything more?

As a result, I developed a minimalist mindset shaped by a deep awareness of mortality – I became someone who doesn't chase more than I need. Though painful at the time, I now see those early experiences as an asset. Sometimes, it's the darkest moments that become the very foundation for a meaningful life.

Let's think of everything you hold now as something that just happened to come your way. Each thing is a gift that has circulated to you through an invisible ecosystem of human society. I believe this ecosystem is one part of the greater law of circulation that governs the natural world. Therefore, you have no need – and no obligation – to cling to any of it. When life feels heavy and painful, you can let go of what is weighing you down and return it to the greater circulation. When you feel a pull toward your next big challenge, you can let go of what no longer serves you. Then you can be lighter, freer and ready for your new adventure.

First, listen to your inner compass – the subconscious awareness of life and death. It asks you fundamental questions each day: 'Why was I born? What am I living for?'

Second, follow the core daily practices of minimalism: let go – clear, simplify, downsize, declutter, streamline and slow down.

In this turbulent world, living by these two principles is the simplest strategy for true happiness.

The Pain of Loss and the Freedom of Letting Go

There is one more truth we must never forget. Even in what we call a peaceful and safe era, there are people being stripped of everything. At this very moment, war, terrorism or natural disasters are forcing them

INTRODUCTION

into a state of 無一物 (*Muichimotsu*) – 'possessing nothing'. This is a heartbreaking reality we must face. And we need to remember that this could happen to you or me as well.

Most of these people are first forced to crawl out of the abyss of despair. Not from nothing, but from far below zero, deep in the negative. Only then can they begin to slowly rebuild a minimal standard of living and reclaim a primal sense of happiness. That demands enormous effort, time and money just to regain what was lost. The pursuit of 'freedom' may come only after that.

Which is harder: letting go of the unnecessary to gain freedom and happiness, or desperately gathering the basics just to survive? Needless to say, the latter is far harder. That question alone triggers intense guilt. And remember – having the freedom to let go by your own will is a luxury and a kind of privilege. It is different from losing or giving up. Letting go doesn't bring pain or sorrow – it brings lightness, clarity and a refreshing relief.

These positive feelings embody the ancient concept of 禊 (*Misogi*) – a purification ritual in Shinto, Japan's indigenous religion. Misogi is the practice of washing away 穢れ (*Kegare*) — the physical excesses and spiritual impurities we naturally accumulate in life.

The essence of Misogi is returning to your pristine, untainted birth state by removing what is unnecessary. It is a sacred ritual of liberation and restoration, for returning to your true self.

The 'Excess Trap' Set by Capitalism

Yet today overwhelming noise keeps flooding in 24/7, confusing you and stealing your focus, your time — your very life itself. Stuff. Services. Social media. Messages. Advice from others. To-dos. News. Ads. This constant overflow clouds your judgement, misleads your mind and exhausts your brain. Then it robs you of the will to choose, distorts your humanity and destroys your freedom. In the end, it even erases who you truly are.

But this is not your fault. It is the trap of our over-consumption society. From your possessions to information. From your thoughts to your relationships. From your work to your daily life. The more you let go of what you don't need, both within and

INTRODUCTION

outside you, the more stress and fatigue fades away.

Let me say it again. The more you let go, the more your freedom and sense of happiness will rise.

Many people say it takes courage to let go of something you've already gained. I understand. But once you learn the mindset and techniques I share in this book, you'll realize that courage is not really necessary.

If you're still hesitant, let me offer you these words: 'You can do anything, but not everything.' It sounds like Zen wisdom, doesn't it? But this quote comes from David Allen, author of the bestseller *Getting Things Done*. This simple phrase reveals the difficulty of choice in life – what to keep and what to let go – and the vital importance of priorities.

It also points to a truth about life-threatening risk. If you keep saying yes to everything and everybody, your days will be buried in trivial matters. In the end, you risk losing your whole life.

The Principle of Minimalism: Letting Go Equals Choosing

Life is far too short to do *everything*, and we only live once. The end often comes suddenly.

Why not spend your limited time – your life itself – on what truly matters?

Maximize what matters most, by minimizing what doesn't matter. By stripping away the unnecessary, the essentials come into view. You begin to remember what you once loved and see what your soul has longed for. As you carve away the excess, your true self –the perfect sculpture that has always been within you – will be revealed. This is your inner artist, who you must protect. (I will explore this throughout the book – it's the underlying theme.)

So how can you tell what is unnecessary in your life? In this overloaded world, this is actually the most difficult question. But don't worry – by reading through this book, you will automatically practise letting the unnecessary things go. As a result, you will feel as light as if you could fly and gain true freedom without courage or fear. You'll realize that you can do anything you love and live

INTRODUCTION

any life you dream of. (But just remember – you can't do everything!)

Keep this in mind: letting go is choosing. What you let go – and what you hold dear – will ultimately design your life.

Freedom begins not in what you gain, but in what you let go.

'Purity is a state of being inwardly free of everything that belongs to this world.'

ST FRANCIS OF ASSISI
Friar (1181/82–1226)

Radical Minimalist
who let go of privilege to pursue an extremely minimal life, following in the footsteps of Christ.

Prologue

Never Let Go of Your Freedom

●

Life is meant to be free. You can do anything you want – as long as you stop chasing *more and more*. Deep down, you know that your time is limited. That's why you want to live without regret.

When you were young there wasn't much that weighed you down. You imagined growing into the adult you wanted to be. You must have dreamed – at least once – of a life filled with joyful work and bright days. Endless fun with friends, exciting challenges and discovering the love of your life.

Giving Up Freedom Is Abandoning Yourself

Yet many people gradually turn into boring adults – those who have lost their dreams and hopes. Because they try to be respectable members of society, they often get stuck in unspoken rules, cultural norms and peer pressure. For example, people who speak of rebellion, yet remain bound by authority and systems. Or people who cling to status and titles, avoiding new challenges.

When you were young, you may have disliked such adults — who only talk but never act, and who defend their own interests and safety. Your inner voice whispered, 'I'll never become like that.'

Meanwhile your rational head shouts, 'Choose stability, don't take risks and secure your career.' But is it really okay to live such a dull life? Does cost-benefit mindset or chasing others' approval bring you joy? Are you happy with a life imposed upon by unfounded 'common sense' and loveless advice?

You once questioned that way of life. One day, you wake up and realize you've become exactly what you never wanted to be. An overburdened and dull version of yourself, no longer free. It has been happening little by little, without you noticing. Don't you think it's strange?

No one truly wants to be chained to invisible hierarchies or preset conditions. We all feel the same yearning to live freely. That feeling never fades, no matter how old we become. Especially in

PROLOGUE

our teenage years, the longing for freedom burns strong. You must have wondered, 'Is there any way to escape the constraints of society?'

But as you enter the workforce, build a business and manage household finances, you begin to feel lost. Swallowed by the unfairness of our money-driven society, you gradually lose your passion, hope and dreams. And eventually, you even forget who you are. How terrifying.

Survival Tactics Learned on the Business Battlefield

I worked for nine years at Sony Music and six years at Warner Music in Tokyo, where fierce competition never sleeps. On the front lines of this profit-obsessed industry, I faced all kinds of unfairness and frustration, just as you have.

I witnessed countless scenes of dragging others down, pointless rivalries and political games for promotion. I endured painful social obligations, aimless meetings and tasks, meaningless long hours and ever-rising sales quotas — all the familiar burdens of corporate life.

LET GO

Yet, I quietly resisted those outdated customs and empty conventions by practising two principles: the art of letting go and minimalist living.

No matter how much my income increased, I maintained my minimalist living throughout my corporate career of fifteen years. My lifestyle was a slight upgrade from my student days, when I lived in a tiny flat and a decades-old van. By keeping that lightness— no matter how much others called me odd behind my back — I defended my freedom. It was my survival tactic against ruthless capitalism and for staying true to my work.

I practised letting go in all kinds of things, big and small. When promotions pushed me far beyond my limits and capacity — along with others' expectations — I let go of my titles and overwork. I did this twice.

The first time was in my late twenties while I was at Sony Music. Overwhelmed by an insane workload, I suffered a nervous breakdown and broke out in hives. I asked to be transferred to a department free from intense pressure. It meant that I voluntarily stepped off the fast track to promotion. People around me were disappointed and some abandoned me. Yet, a year later, I met a rookie R&B duo and turned them into superstars who set multiple sales records that remain unbroken.

The second time was in my mid-thirties. Warner Music had scouted me as head of the production department, but the stress was brutal. I cracked my teeth from severe jaw-clenching and suffered facial paralysis. Unable to do good work, I requested a demotion. As expected, I faced a storm of criticism and ridicule. However, about a year after I returned to the floor as a producer, I signed two incredibly talented newcomers — a female singer and a rock band. From then on, I began creating hit after hit.

The Gift That Came After Choosing to Demote Myself

Everything started to change after I let go of the heavy baggage of promotion and career advancement. I spent more time fly fishing — my lifelong passion — and this dramatically increased my happiness in everyday life. Over about a year, as my mental and physical health improved, I found myself achieving better results at work. Even more surprisingly, an unexpected bonus followed: my income actually increased. The same flow – the same pattern – emerged both times.

Through these experiences, I came to notice what I now call the Law of Letting Go. Whenever you let go of what weighs you down, something even more meaningful will be brought to you – sometimes with a delayed little bonus on top.

However, there is one absolute rule of this law: *you must let go first*. Think of an overworked person as a trekker on a steep trail with an overloaded backpack. All their energy goes into just walking – they are too exhausted to look up at the magnificent view in the distance. They are also too tired to bend down and enjoy the rare alpine flowers at their feet. When you are burdened, you can neither notice nor seize the opportunities right in front of you. And of course, a trekker like that won't even reach the summit.

According to the Law of Letting Go, what you release always returns in a greater form. Once you trust this law, life begins to flow smoothly. Lighten your load and step into a life of freedom. Create enough space physically and mentally to notice, seize opportunities. This is a message I will share

PROLOGUE

with you again and again, leading you towards authentic well-being.

So you shouldn't be afraid of your income or position dropping temporarily. Most people, driven by that fear, end up avoiding challenges – and never become free in life. After all, we now live in a hundred-year life era, unlike the postwar period when the average lifespan was in the fifties. That's why we should never fear shifting down or starting over in our much longer careers. That means you can let go of the anxious rush that can ruin both you and your life.

I was saved by the Law of Letting Go three more times after this. I became convinced that you can feel true happiness only when you choose true freedom. Only then does your true power awaken – your inner artist. Once released, your highest potential brings even greater gifts back to you. My own life is living proof of that.

Research from Harvard University and UCLA shows that happier people are about 30 per cent more productive and three times more creative. This is how the Law of Letting Go works: letting go first, freedom second, happiness third. Then, performance fourth and success fifth. Even so, most people still believe success must come before happiness. They chase success and postpone daily happiness, just like the overloaded trekker I described earlier.

I spent many years in the intense world of the music industry. But by practising those two principles of minimalism – the art of letting go and minimalist living – I was able to work freely. That's how I protect myself from being lost or crushed. Without noticing, I fell deeply in love with music, with artists and with my work itself. In time, people began calling me a hitmaker.

The Vast Freedom Beyond Letting Go of Everything

I could have held on to a stable job, a decent income, status and influential connections. Yet, in 2010, as I was approaching forty, I let go of it all.

To seek true freedom and to fulfil a long-held dream from my student days, I quit my job and moved to New Zealand. I landed there with only a suitcase, a large backpack and a long fly-fishing-rod

PROLOGUE

case. I had no house, no car, and for the first six months I lived in a lakeside campground.

After that, I moved to a basic, wooden house by a remote lake in the forest where I still live today. I spent nearly all the money I had saved through minimalist living.

In the first year, my income dropped to one-tenth of what it had been. Through off-grid and self-sufficient lifestyle my minimalist living evolved even further. As a result, I became free to work without being tied to money.

From there and throughout my forties, I devoted myself to building a work style unbound by organization, location, time or money. Eventually, I fulfilled my ideal lifestyle of extreme freedom through a combination of forest life and nomadic life.

In forest life, I rose with the dawn and rested at sunset, living in rhythm with nature. I lived on spring water, organic vegetables and fruits from my garden, wild forest harvests and freshly caught fish. This self-sufficient life minimized both my environmental impact and living expenses. I spent nearly half the year in my nomadic life, travelling around the world freely as a leading Japanese digital nomad. Whether in the lakeside forest or moving from city to city, I accessed the information I needed and worked on what I love online.

Some people called it an enviable lifestyle, yet nomadic life was hectic and physically demanding – far from easy. Neither your salary nor your future is guaranteed.

Likewise, my forest life – with no water supply, no mobile phone signal, frequent power outages and occasional road closures caused by natural disasters – was never easy.

Still, during that decade of my forties, I helped spark both the digital-nomad boom and the minimalist boom. I also led the trekking and organic movements in Japan. Thanks to my being a pioneer of those social trends, offers of work kept growing.

In those days, my work covered many fields. These included: outside director and advisor for several companies, producing a few brands, developing fly-fishing and trekking gear, supporting ethical apparel, media writing and authoring books. Ninety per cent of my work could be done online – location-free and not tied to fixed hours. The remaining work was location dependent, but I truly loved it – outdoor photo and film shoots, university lectures, producing music festivals, and retreat tours.

Both my liberated work style and the social movements I led were the third cycle of the Law of Letting Go. A great return that came only because I had let go of almost everything else.

A Future I Never Imagined – After Letting Go of Even More

In 2019 – in my tenth year after moving to New Zealand, just a year before the COVID-19 pandemic struck – something unexpected happened in my life.

Looking back, I realized the previous year had been my busiest, with the highest income. Not a single job had been taken for the money – all I wanted was to work freely on only what I loved.

So first, I declared a pause on my nomadic life and let go of all the location-dependent work I was passionate about. (People often asked if I had foreseen the pandemic, but it was pure coincidence.) Next, I let go of all location-free work that paid well but no longer gave me joy. I kept only two things. One was writing – only books, not even articles – which had become my *Ikigai*, my reason for living. The other was managing LifestyleDesign. Camp, an online community I loved.

As a result of letting go of busyness, my income was cut in half. But in exchange, I tripled the size of our vegetable garden and planted thirty new fruit trees. Furthermore, beyond my expertize in lake fly fishing, I mastered sea kayak fishing. These efforts drastically improved our household self-sufficiency. With minimal expenses, I finally achieved my long-held vision: the forest life where my family of three could live slowly, and fully (I became a father in my fifties – the greatest miracle of letting go!)

No longer chased by work, I could now devote almost all of my time to what I truly loved: my family, self-sufficiency and authoring books. Eventually, I created what I call ultimate minimalist living – a life strategy that minimizes the impact of severe inflation, economic crises, pandemics and wars in the outside world.

Then, the two books I had spent four to five years writing both became bestsellers. Even though my working hours had been cut by more than half, my income quietly returned. This miraculous reward was the fourth cycle of the Law of Letting Go.

That's why I can let go of so-called 'big things' without fear or courage. Whenever I devote myself to what matters most without compromise, life rewards me. That's how it works. But many say, 'That is too idealistic.' Let me say it again. Even if the world feels harsh and unfair, many of us have access to prosperity and freedom like never before. Simply stop trying to do everything and step forward focusing only on what you truly love. You can create *a life that's your own.*

The key lies in how much you can let go – or how much you can't. You don't need to let go as radically as I did. But, in this age of mass consumption, many people carry far more than they need, believing that they must have more and more to achieve true wealth and happiness.

The Freest Person Is the One Who Has Nothing to Lose

Some people believe that we should gain as much as we can and keep growing more and more. But greater danger lies in our endless hunger to acquire everything. More connections, more possessions, more information, more apps, more qualifications. Before long, excess weighs us down, and we lose sight of who we truly are. This is the sickness of never-ending growth.

When I was young, people told me over and over: 'If you want to succeed, be more ambitious.'

'To win, you have to be stronger and aim higher.' I nearly gave in to such ruthless advice, but I refused to be swallowed by it. It was tough and painful. Looking back, I now see that those struggles preserved my freedom and my true self.

Why was I able to resist? Since childhood, I had been mentally fragile. Until my forties, I suffered from social anxiety and lacked the courage to speak up for myself. So why?

Because I was saved by the principles of minimalism. No matter how much I earned or how high I rose, I never tried to live bigger. In fact, I've lowered my living costs as I've grown older. I let go of things – both big and small – without hesitation. My strategy of minimalist living and the art of letting go brought me a state of having nothing to lose.

Ultimately, those who have nothing to lose – and who aren't afraid to let go – are the strongest.

That's why I could lightly refuse what didn't feel right and take steady steps despite opposition. I've stayed highly focused and creative for over twenty-five years, well into my mid-fifties. The results speak for themselves.

Revealing the True Self Beneath the Excess

Some young people today – less materialistic, less ambitious, and less interested in networking – are often criticized for 'lacking drive'. But I don't think they're wrong. When you try to do everything and keep adding options, your efforts and results become scattered. In the end, you waste what's most precious– your life itself.

Let go freely. Focus drastically.

LET GO

First, let go of the impatience whispering, 'I must achieve big things while I'm young.' Next, let go of the pressure saying, 'I want to succeed before they do.' When you do this, you release the heaviest burden we all carry – the excessive expectations you place on yourself. Then, let go of what doesn't matter in your life nor leads you closer to your real dreams. This includes comparison, obsession with reputation and the winner–loser mindset. These external standards gradually erase your happiness and true self.

The more you let go, the more the noise fades from your sight and your mind. You become unburdened again, like a child, and what you love most becomes clear. The more you let go, the more your concentration and sensitivity sharpen. Your creativity and performance rise, and your hidden abilities are activated to their fullest potential.

Simplicity tends to become featureless, but true minimalism makes a feature stand out. By carving away the excess, you set free the one and only artist within. This, indeed, is *Misogi* – purification through letting go.

Let go of 'just in case' thinking and make the bold decision to focus on what matters most. That

PROLOGUE

singular focus is the only path to freedom. For me, that is how I have lived freely and happily. Now, at fifty-five, living in my family of three, that philosophy remains unchanged and always will. Stay true to yourself.

Regain your inner life force – the sense of wonder and adventure you once had as a child. Then walk your own path, freely and gracefully – on your own terms.

'A table, a chair, a bowl of fruit and a violin; what else does a man need to be happy?'

ALBERT EINSTEIN
Theoretical physicist (1879–1955)

Minimalist of Clarity
who let go of luxury and social expectations to live
simply and think freely.

STEP 1

•

Money & Belongings

WHAT DO YOU NEED TO GAIN FREEDOM?

You don't need to possess much – only the decisiveness to let go of what you don't need. The more you let go of, the more clearly you'll see what truly matters. Little by little, your authentic self will be carved out. Don't be afraid to have few belongings or empty your space. The comfort of living with nothing but what you love will give you mental room and spark your creativity. What about money? It's the same as with your belongings – you only need the minimum to be free.

1

Let go of the noise in your vision

●

LEAD A SIMPLE AND CREATIVE LIFE
Do not allow even the smallest distraction.

Things slowly and steadily creep into your space without you noticing. Things that no longer fit on crowded shelves. Things stacked on the floor. Things tucked into drawers or left out on tables.

Maybe you told yourself you'd organize them some day, or that they might be useful. But take a closer look. When was the last time you used them?

Everything except the things you love is visual noise.

Noise in your vision not only clutters up your physical space, but also complicates your mind and

LET GO

your lifestyle. Many people are too tolerant of this noise. Yet they say they want an even bigger home or a larger office. Unless they change their habits, even a more spacious house or workplace will only fill their life with more noise.

Let's do an experiment right now. It's time to reset your desk.

Clean off everything except your laptop and your favourite cup. If possible, move your desk closer to a window. It's okay if you don't have the best view in the world. Turn your attention to the sunlight and the presence of the vast sky beyond the window. Even in a big city, these are precious moments of nature that you can still feel. They are the essence of serenity — the opposite of noise

When you rid noise from your space, your thoughts suddenly sharpen. You begin to feel like working on important projects you've been putting off. Once you start, time flies. It will spark joy in your heart and fill you with vibrant energy.

This is what we call sacred creative time. How much you have of it determines the quality of your life.

LET GO OF THE NOISE IN YOUR VISION

To see dramatic change in your life, first you need to have some simple space.

●

SHIFT from
'I'll put it away someday'
to
'I'll clear it away now'.

2

Let go of what you aren't using

●

THE BEAUTY OF NOTHING
Saying goodbye to things is a farewell
to your past self.

Each object in your space is something you once chose to buy or receive. Some you may feel quite attached to emotionally, and some would be very hard to let go of. No one would blame you for thinking, 'I might find a use for this someday'. You might make excuses driven by fear, such as 'What if I can never get this again?', and end up holding on to such things for the rest of your life.

Here is one fundamental minimalist mindset: let go of anything you're not using regularly right now.

Then shape your own rule around this extremely simple mindset. 'Does it spark joy?' 'Would I pay for it again?' 'Do I really need this – not just want to keep it?' 'Have I used it through all four seasons?' What matters most is having a clear rule of your own, so you become more decisive each time you let go.

You can sell it, give it away or throw it out. Aside from items with emotional significance, there's little that you can't do without. If you're not sure whether to keep something or not, just let it go. Priorities in life are constantly changing, and therefore the items you need will change constantly too.

Do the first huge clean-up all in one go. Ideally, complete it over a weekend. If that is difficult, use a long weekend or add paid leave to the weekend to finish it in three to four days. After that, do a thorough review about once a year, taking a one-day block to do so. In Japan, this is typically done around the New Year's holidays as a symbolic way to clear out your soul before the start of a fresh new year. It's the perfect time to take an inventory of your belongings.

With most items, the basic rule is to decide on the spot whether to let them go or keep them. But sentimental items are different. Because they are full of memories, it is hard to judge them quickly. For things you don't use or display anymore but that are filled with deep memories, the only solution is to let time help you decide. You can gradually reduce the number of items with emotional significance. There's no rush, so you can take your time, even if it means many years.

Start by collecting them into a 'memory box' and put it somewhere you won't see it every day. Once a year, open the box and look through everything. When an item no longer stirs such strong feelings in you, that is the time to let it go. Say goodbye to them one at a time, little by little. You can scan pictures and letters, and take photos or short videos of things such as drawings or bigger objects to have a record of them.

Ideally, you will keep all these sentimental items in just one memory box. If you have a lot of them, prepare several boxes for different periods of your life – for example, one for drawings you made in school and another for letters you exchanged with a friend in your early twenties. As the years pass, your big box (or boxes) of items will slowly become smaller. Each time you let something go, let go of

LET GO

the sadness and guilt you feel about throwing it away, too.

If you still find it hard to let go, I'd like to share a line from Japan's most famous contemporary author, whom I deeply respect, Haruki Murakami: 'You have to let go of the past that is gone.' Keep asking yourself whether you intend to take these items to the grave with you. Remember that you were born with nothing and will leave this world with nothing.

The goal here is to create a simple space with no disturbance, just your favourite music playing gently in the background. It's easier than you think to create a relaxing atmosphere like in a peaceful hotel room or sophisticated café and a comfortable space with enough room for your thoughts to breathe and your creativity to shine.

●

SHIFT from
'For now, I guess I'll keep it'
to
'For now, I'll say goodbye'.

3

Let go of the need to stock up

●

GOING MINIMAL

Use a storage facility.

Imagine the moment you want to use something, you've run out and have none left. That may seem annoying, or even scary.

It's true that not stocking up means buying items whenever you run out. Buying in bulk may seem smarter, but how often does buying less cause a major problem? Do you always use up everything you buy in bulk without wasting it?

Items you buy in bulk or rarely use end up occupying or cluttering your home and work space. You waste money on space to store them. They also drain your energy and time trying to use them up, organize them or search for items.

Except for emergency supplies for natural disasters, you really do not have to stock up. Almost anything you need can be bought, ordered or rented when required.

Try thinking of your neighbourhood supermarket as an extension of your own refrigerator, and consider online retailers as your personal giant storage facility. You can break free from the habit of overstocking everyday items. Think of these businesses as services that keep a huge number of products on your behalf for a few cents a day. You can order from or visit them whenever you need something. This frees you from the anxiety of thinking you have to buy everything in advance. You stop wasting time, energy and money managing items. This creates space in both your sight and your mind — and your spirit naturally settles. As a result, you begin to reconnect with yourself.

Having less in your cupboards and closets also means you spend less time thinking about how to organize things, creating space for you to see yourself for who you really are. Choosing not to

LET GO OF THE NEED TO STOCK UP

store things indiscriminately is a way for you to nurture your own heart and mind.

●

SHIFT from
'I'd better buy a lot in advance'
to
'I'll get it when I need it'.

4

Let go of your stingy habits

●

PAY IT FORWARD

Give to those who need it more.

Things, people, work, information and money — all need to circulate. If anything stays in one place too long, it will gradually become stagnant. Eventually it will cloud your thoughts and even your life.

Just as flowing water circulates in nature, the CO_2 in the air humans breathe out returns to plants and transforms into oxygen. In the same way, we can let go of all kinds of things around us to those who need them more, creating healthy circulation.

If you have tools that you no longer use, find someone who would be happy to use them. If there

LET GO

is someone better suited for the work you're doing now, let them do it. When an opportunity comes along, give it to someone who has been waiting for it even longer than you. When you meet a wonderful person, introduce them to someone you know they'd connect with on an even deeper level. When you have a great idea, tell someone who you know would be able to make the most of it, even more than you.

You may worry that acting this way will eventually mean you'll have nothing left. But remember, we came into this world with nothing when we were born. You don't have to expect anything in return. You just let go first. The more you give away, the more new things come in to fill the space created. And very often, you end up receiving things you truly needed. Instead of going out looking for them, wonderful things come to you.

Opportunities and money are always circulating within the invisible ecosystem of human society. In this circulation the total value they hold remains constant. The most important thing is to always be clear about what you really love and to keep on sharing that with other people. This elegant ecosystem is a part of the greater law of circulation that governs the natural world. It is designed to guide everything towards the people who need it most.

●

SHIFT from
'I'll give you this in exchange for that'
to
'Here, this one's on me'.

5

Let go of small purchases

●

A LITTLE MAKES A BIG LOSS
Small expenses you hardly notice can do more harm than big spending you choose.

What's robbing you of real financial freedom is not just luxury spending like meals out and buying expensive clothing, but cheap daily items like bottled drinks, gum, candy and subscriptions that renew without even thinking about it. The root cause behind the vague money stress you always feel is not the expensive items you intend to buy. It's the build-up of many small things that you don't even remember buying. We tend to put off spending money on the big things we actually need. Yet we end up spending far more on small things we don't even need, just for a brief hit of pleasure.

What can we do about this? I recommend creating a personal rule to help you decide what or what not to buy. For example, I decided not to buy plastic bottles smaller than 500ml – instead I carry around my own favourite reusable water bottle for daily use. And if I'm being honest, no plastic drinks bottle is designed beautifully enough to motivate me to carry it.

Another idea is to build a system that naturally protects you from small, unnecessary spending. Back in the days before digital payments were everywhere, the main problem was coins. People tend to feel a kind of weight when they hand over paper notes, even though they are physically light. Yet they somehow treat coins lightly, even though they are heavier. Maybe because of that, when your wallet is full of loose change, you end up buying small, unnecessary things without thinking. At that time, I recommended people to let go of their big, thick wallets with coin purses and instead use a small, thin wallet or money clip that only holds notes. That's what I was doing too.

LET GO OF SMALL PURCHASES

Over the past several years, as digital payments have become the norm, I have started recommending a minimal wallet that attaches to your smartphone and holds only a few cards. But now that we no longer need coins or even cards, and we can pay almost anywhere with a single tap of a smartphone, impulse buying has actually increased. Notes and coins are physical objects, which at least gave us a physical sense of paying. Virtual digital payments do not give us that feeling at all. That is why they are so dangerous.

Your smartphone is a small monster that steals your attention and your time – and now it steals your money as well. So how can we resist this digital black magic that robs us of the feeling of paying? Let me share the system I am using right now to fight back.

First, for everyday life, I link my smartphone payments to a debit card that takes money from my bank account immediately. That makes each payment feel more real than with a credit card, where the bill arrives in a lump sum later. Make sure to limit yourself to just one card.

I also set things up so that every time I pay, I get an instant notification on my phone. While I usually turn off almost all notifications (except for calls, important calendar alerts and one chat app for essential contacts), I keep the payment notifications turned on. These give me a clear sense that I have just paid for something and also prompt a brief inner review of whether that purchase was really necessary.

Of course, this system is far from perfect. AI has now entered the scene, and the digital world keeps advancing. There is no small trick to completely resist it. In the end, the most powerful and effective way to protect yourself is to go back to the basics.

Whenever you feel the urge to buy, stop and ask your inner voice, 'Could I talk to someone about this passionately?' If not, don't buy it, even if it only costs a dollar. Every time one more thing comes into your life, you lose a little bit of freedom. You must not forget that cause and effect. If you still decide to get it after checking against this basic question, that thing — no matter how cheap or expensive it is — will make you shine. People who live only with things they love are truly attractive, with a rare beauty.

LET GO OF SMALL PURCHASES

SHIFT from
'I feel uneasy without it'
to
'I'm perfectly fine without it'.

'Perfection is achieved,
not when there is
nothing more to add,
but when there is nothing
left to take away.'

ANTOINE DE SAINT-EXUPÉRY

Author of The Little Prince and the Aviator
(1900–1944)

Minimalist of the Essential
who let go of comfort to search in the sky for the
truth of the human heart.

6

Let go of impulse shopping

●

LISTEN TO YOUR SOUL
Only buy things you truly love.

Shopping is a project that exists to enrich and free your life. When you come across something you really want – just wait for a moment.

First, ask yourself if buying it would be an investment, an expense or a waste of money. If it feels worth more than what you paid, it's an investment. If it feels equal, it's an expense. If it feels lower than the price, it's a waste.

This holds true even if what you want to buy only costs a dollar. People who don't think twice about spending small amounts of money often end up losing the most. There is a saying in Japanese that fits that type of person perfectly: 'A person who laughs at one yen will also cry over one yen.'

Once you feel like buying something, the next step is not to pay with a single smartphone tap or click 'buy now', but to do deep research as if you were a scholar or an expert about that item. Start by checking the facts about the item: its specifications, its materials, who made it and how it was made. Then see how well it matches your own criteria. I recommend three simple questions: Why do you need it (not just want it)? How will you use it? What truly matters in your life? If you feel satisfied with that, then look for reviews from people who actually use it in their daily lives. But be careful. Avoid any information that is advertising, even if it is posted by an individual.

My personal criteria is that it must be beautiful, minimal or innovative. If possible, it should also be lightweight and compact. Ideally, it should also have more than one function and be foldable, stackable or easy to store. I also seriously consider the impact: will this significantly elevate my abilities or expand my possibilities?

LET GO OF IMPULSE SHOPPING

After all that, if you still feel confident that you need it, go home and sleep on it. The next morning, when you wake up and still feel the same way, you'll go back to the store – even if it's a hassle. When you pick up the item in your hands, if it moves your heart, buy it. Even if it's sold out, you won't die. Just wait for the next chance.

The cities we live in today are designed to make us buy things. Many of the things we want are triggered by outside noise – advertising, trends or competition. They often turn out to be things we don't need at all. Listen to your inner voice from your soul which tells you what you truly need. Ignore your head filled with endless desire and outside information.

Seek out only what fits your sense of beauty. Then buy only what you love enough to talk about for more than ten minutes.

●

SHIFT from
'I'll miss out if I don't buy this now'
to
'Not rushing to buy it was the right choice'.

7
Let go of not being choosy

●

YOU ARE WHAT YOU BUY
It's not about what you save, it's about what you choose.

Feeling stress or anxiety about money is very common, but that doesn't mean you should be trying to save and cut back on every single thing. Whether it's dieting, studying or anything we don't truly want to do, our brains aren't designed to endure constant perseverance and self-denial. The harder you try to resist spending by saving and scrimping, the more likely your mind will rebel — often with a burst of spending.

Just because a lunch is cheap doesn't make

it better. Entertainment that doesn't cost much money isn't necessarily the best. It doesn't matter if you're getting a better deal than other people or if you're buying something on sale. What's important isn't how much you save but how well you choose.

Saving money just for the sake of saving never lasts. Make your goal crystal clear, and choose as if you were investing part of your life. Even in a half-price sale, buying something you had never even wanted before is not only a waste of money but also disrespectful of your own precious life. Even buying something as casual as flip-flops requires serious consideration and not a careless choice just because the price looks like a deal.

If someone asks what you want to eat, be ready with a clear answer that reflects what you truly want – don't just go along with whatever. Letting others choose for you is easier than making decisions, but you are paying the price of no longer sitting in the driver's seat of your own life.

What do you truly want to do? What things do you actually want? If you can't give an honest answer to these kinds of questions, eventually you'll lose sight of who you truly are.

LET GO OF NOT BEING CHOOSY

Try making a list of things you really like in every category you can think of. Look over it frequently so that you can own your choices and voice them clearly. This will help you see who you truly are and what you truly want to do.

●

SHIFT from
'I bought it because it's cheap'
to
'I bought it because it's exactly what I wanted'.

8

Let go of accessorizing

●

NATURAL BEAUTY IS REAL BEAUTY
Instead of adding extras, appreciate the standard version.

'Simplicity is the ultimate sophistication.' This popular saying is widely – though never definitively – attributed to Leonardo da Vinci.

Sometimes you feel vaguely lonely or anxious, or your confidence and self-esteem are low. Then you start adding things, buying items or surrounding yourself with more and more stuff. But no matter how much you decorate with things, they can never fill a hole inside or make you shine. Others can easily sense when it is just decoration and not your true self.

And on top of that, when you add decorations or extra pieces to things, they usually end up more awkward to use. Remember that a thing exists to serve its owner. The things you own come to life when you use them fully with love and purpose, until they are worn by time, as if they were part of you, gently enriching your days.

I've always bought used cars – my current car is already twenty years old. Because I often drive on rough roads deep in the forest or mountainside, they always end up battered and worn. I have shown my love by driving each car hard, until beyond repair. To me, my car has never been a decorative item or a status symbol – it has always been my lovely companion that carries me into the wild.

If my jeans fit my body well, I never wear a belt. A carrot picked fresh from my garden tastes perfect raw and needs no cooking or seasoning. A solid wood table has a natural beauty and looks best without a tablecloth or plastic sheet. When something is well made, extra options, toppings and decorations are not always necessary.

The iPhone was designed as a piece of minimal art and looks most beautiful when it is naked. To

LET GO OF ACCESSORIZING

maximize the appeal of the Apple logo, everything else has been carved away to the limit. This reflects Steve Jobs's aesthetic as the founder of Apple. At the same time, an expensive and fragile iPhone may need some protection. I gently encourage you to look for a simple cover or thin bumper that is as light as possible, while keeping the iPhone's raw beauty. Try to find one only for protection, not for extra decoration. Take this as a lesson in minimalism.

But if you truly fall in love with a particular decorative case, then go for it, no matter how thick, heavy or expensive it is. It will help you shine not from the outside, but from inside. After all, the purpose of this book is not only to share ways to minimize what is unnecessary in your life, but also to remind you of the importance of maximizing what truly matters to you: inner freedom, the joy of life and your own happiness.

The more unnecessary decorations you add, the more they muddy and hide an item's authenticity. Here is one truth of minimalism: the more excess that is removed, the more value and beauty that is reclaimed. The same is true for people. By letting go of superfluous decorations, you restore the pure

LET GO

and natural beauty you were born with, and your originality stands out.

One of the most famous Japanese minimalists and my long-time friend, whom I call the Minimalist of Joy, Marie Kondo, often says that 'letting go is more important than adding'. Enjoy letting go instead of adding. It will make you feel much lighter, both physically and mentally — and that is true freedom.

●

SHIFT from
***'I want this to impress others
or fill the emptiness inside'***
to
***'I want to use this fully and
get the most value from it'.***

9

Let go of chasing a bigger life

●

WORK OUT YOUR MINIMUM LIVING COST

Become emotionally free from money.

When people start working, get promoted or change jobs and earn more money, they often tend to upgrade their lifestyles more and more. What we often overlook is that when you raise just one part of your lifestyle, your total monthly or even yearly expenses go up, not just as a one-time cost. This means that even a slight drop in income can throw your whole life out of balance.

We become so afraid of this imbalance that even small changes in our income put us on an emotional roller coaster. We end up stuck in a cycle of fear and become boring adults, desperate only to protect our stability.

In order to be free from money, start playing with the idea of your 'minimum living cost'. How much would it cost you to live for a year at the bare minimum? How much do you need to pay for yourself or your family to have healthy meals, comfortable clothes for each season and a safe place to sleep? If you can calculate that, you'll know exactly when you can afford to fully commit when it really counts. I'm not a hippie or a monk saying you don't need money – you only need enough to be happy.

People are often scared to take on big challenges because of a vague fear of losing something. Is there really meaning in a life where you never take on a challenge? If you can clarify what you're afraid of losing, you can devote your whole self to your life and work without compromising or selling out. And in a worst-case scenario, you can always go back to the starting line.

You never know when big opportunities and critical moments will come. It's important to prepare for them by reducing your minimum living cost to as low as possible while you can. Stay aware of invisible spending that regularly drains your money for no good reason. Cancel any subscriptions or contracts that are no longer useful. This is your chance to look back, find the bad spending habits behind those invisible small expenses. You'll be amazed at how clearly they reveal your past self. Let them go completely. I'm not telling you to be miserly or cheap. Minimalist living is the most rational strategy for financial freedom in this uncertain society. In other words, it's a non-violent, creative form of rebellion against the hyper-capitalist system.

The moment you can tell yourself that you'll be fine no matter what happens in life, you will be free from money.

●

SHIFT from
'Upgrading your lifestyle when your income rises'
to
'Choosing your lifestyle based on your own values'.

10

Let go of having too many clothes

●

FIND YOUR BEST FIT

Decide on your personal staple items.

What comes to mind when you think of your most worn clothing items?

'This one's for everyday wear, this one is for bedtime, this is for formal occasions ...' Taken to extremes, you could limit your wardrobe to the best outfit for each category and just wear those items repeatedly. Most of us already tend to wear our favourites the most. When you come across something that feels more like an expression of who you are, you can replace the old favourite with a new one. Try letting go of the clothes that are 'just okay', and leave only the perfect

LET GO

outfits in your closet. If you are fortunate enough to come across the ultimate staple clothing or outfit, think about spending as much as you can afford on it.

What colours, types of material and shapes truly excite you in your wardrobe? What suits your body type, facial features and skin, hair and eye colour the most? Be so thorough in your physical examination that others may find it silly and laugh at how seriously you're taking this. Take your time, get on your feet and search for a style that truly suits you.

When a style you wear feels right you feel confidence and ease. Your mind becomes clearer, and your thinking more creative. Others will feel it through the energy you quietly radiate.

There's no need to feel bad about your current body type. There are clothes out there that flatter each body type. Even actors and pop stars come in various shapes and sizes – not everybody is built like a supermodel. They shine on stage because they've found their own timeless wardrobe essentials – pieces that suit their natural shape – and they continue to work hard to look the best they can, using the body they were born with.

LET GO OF HAVING TOO MANY CLOTHES

The vast majority of my wardrobe is made up of simple outfits and outdoor clothing that have nothing to do with popular trends. Simple clothes in plain, flattering colours never go out of style, and outdoor wear is tough, lightweight and highly functional. They're comfortable and easy to move around in. Designs that achieve beauty through functionality are the best.

In the mountains, trekkers like me often face four seasons in one day, and sometimes even life-threatening conditions. I love outdoor wear because it can withstand storms and keep my body warm and dry in rapidly changing weather. It also never goes out of style and can be an all-year-round staple.

●

SHIFT from
'I want to buy new clothes because I got bored of mine'
to
'I'm going to buy clothes I'll never get tired of'.

'The more you know,
the less you need.'

YVON CHOUINARD
Founder of Patagonia and climber (born 1938)

Minimalist of Responsibility
who let go of excess consumption to pursue a
responsible way of living and business.

STEP 2

•

Work

Difficult work can be fun and interesting but, in order to take it on, you need to create both the time and emotional space to handle it. People who thoroughly enjoy the work they do, without exception, are always conscious of wasted time and actions that take away from it. They abandon any work that isn't actually useful. If you want to focus on what matters most, you have to be disciplined about cutting out everything that doesn't matter. Give yourself the permission to make time for the work you truly want to do.

11

Let go of work you're not good at

●

MAKE YOUR TIME CREATIVE TIME

Complete small tasks sincerely and quickly using smart tools and full focus.

It may be beautiful when you care deeply about your work and pay full attention to all the details. However, the attitude that you have to do everything yourself reduces productivity and can hold the whole team back.

People who work with an inner freedom that is true to themselves are good at sharing the load, because they understand their own strengths and weaknesses. They naturally develop the habit of finding their role in a team, and this, in turn, keeps

LET GO

them aware of the team as a whole.

They know they shouldn't do everything themselves for the sake of the team.

When they face tasks they are bad at or don't know how to handle, they politely ask for help and respectfully hand those tasks over to others. Because of this, they can focus their time and energy on the work they are good at or passionate about. This is the secret behind their high performance and how they truly contribute to the team.

Consider it your duty to focus on the work you really should be doing, and let others help you with the tasks they can do better. The task you've been struggling with might be something that another person who has talent and works at a high level in that area can finish in no time.

If there's still work left, it will often be small tasks or chores. Don't underestimate these and never treat them carelessly. Engage with full focus and creativity. Dive into tasks with a sincere heart, and make full use of tools, devices, systems and apps to work as efficiently as possible and finish in the shortest time. That way, you can create as much of your own beautiful time as possible – time to focus only on the work you are truly meant to do.

Take everything you gain by putting what you've learned in this lesson into practice – the time, energy and mental space you free up. Then invest all of it in work where you can make full use of your originality and in making your long-term vision real. Keep focusing on the work that no one else but you can do, and keep offering it to society. That is the true definition of 'work'.

The reason you were born is to pursue your authenticity and dreams until your time runs out and your life comes to an end. No matter what your job or title is, you can always step onto your own path in life.

●

SHIFT from
'Trying to do everything yourself'
to
'Focusing your energy where it truly counts'.

12

Let go of the multitasking mindset

●

KEEP YOUR FOCUS

As in a traditional matcha ceremony, focus on what is in front of you now.

The bad habit of constantly thinking ahead is a distraction to the mind. It has the power to ruin your life.

While enjoying some delicious food, you think about what you're going to eat next. While working, you think about where to go for a drink after five. You take lots of pictures of the scenery without actually looking at it, thinking to enjoy the photos later.

No matter how beautiful the world in front of you, you won't see, hear or feel it if your mind is elsewhere.

LET GO

'If you chase two rabbits, you will catch neither' – this is an old saying from ancient China. 'To do two things at once is to do neither' is a similar saying from ancient Rome. In my own words: 'You can't climb two mountains at once.' This simple truth can be found in every age and every culture. Research from Harvard backs this up: multitasking doesn't improve efficiency – it harms the brain and significantly reduces productivity.

Early in my career, I worked with a top performer on our team who seemed able to juggle many things at once. When I observed him closely, I realized his method was straightforward and clear. He simply wrote down everything he needed to do. Then he lined them up in order of priority and did them one at a time from the top down. When he was working on one task, he didn't even glance at the second, third or any subsequent things on that list.

Because he only ever focused on one thing at a time, he completed his work much more quickly, and to a higher standard, too. As a result, he delivered high-quality work at a rapid pace – seeming to do many things at once when, in fact, it was always just one at a time. It is a simple principle.

He was able to clearly distinguish between two ways of seeing his work. One was the bird's eye view of looking over everything that needed to be done. The other was the worm's eye view, giving his full attention only to the task in front of him in that moment.

So turn your focus on what you need to be doing right now. Don't run around trying to do everything at once, skipping from one task to another. Just finish one thing at a time. Gently bring your drifting mind back from whatever is worrying you, and return your full presence to what's in front of you. You can face the worry later – the worry can wait.

The most important thing you have is not tomorrow, nor is it yesterday. It is the moment you have right now, right here. Observe carefully and feel deeply. Savour the moment now, nothing else. Once you enter into this feeling, you transform into the artist you really are, and you unleash your incredible power.

LET GO

●

SHIFT from
'What's coming up next?'
to
'Right now, this is everything'.

13

Let go of your thirst for recognition

•

LOOK AFTER YOURSELF

No successful person gives optimistic estimates.

'I'll do it right away.' 'Leave it to me.'

When you respond to someone with enthusiasm, the other person will usually be pleased.

When you're young, that might work well enough. But as you grow older, there are times when that same attitude can backfire. I know this well, because I've experienced it myself.

Sometimes you may feel you have to bluff in order to grab the work you want most. You may be tempted to commit to an unrealistic deadline or quickly say, 'Sure, I can do that!' This happens even though deep down you recognize it might be impossible. Overpromising is already a betrayal of the other person's trust.

It's dangerous to promise too much and attempt to get through a task with sheer willpower alone. You will only burden and exhaust yourself later. When you continue to do this as a habit, eventually you'll see yourself as a failure – a person who can only say yes and make empty promises. That's what I was like in my early years working at that company.

Make it a habit to always write down the amount of work you have to do and your worries about it all. It's easy to say yes to anything that's asked of you, but it's very hard to say no. In order for you to respond correctly, you need to make sure you have a complete grasp of the weight of the burden you're already carrying.

You might feel hesitant to tell someone no, say sorry or that you can't do what they need you to do, because you don't want to let the other person down. But find the courage to tell them the reality of your situation as quickly as possible, even if it might disappoint them.

LET GO OF YOUR THIRST FOR RECOGNITION

What people really expect from you at work is not reckless overwork, but the ability to reliably turn projects in on time. A person who can do that doesn't need to be managed – and good leaders know it.

●

SHIFT from

'Trying to prove your effort'

to

'Making sure you do quality work'.

14

Let go of your to-do list

●

LIVE YOUR LIFE

Is this really yours to do?

How many of those 'really important things' on your to-do list would risk your life if you didn't do them immediately?

Sometimes, when you're busy, you suddenly realize you have become obsessed with adding more and more items to your to-do list and crossing items off. This feeling is easy to understand. By increasing the number of things you need to do, you ease the anxiety of having nothing to do. The simple act of crossing items off the list gives you a subtle sense of pleasure.

LET GO

But to-do items that are not directly related to your goals and what matters most to you are just noise in your life. You become tied to the to-do list. Checking items off the list becomes your whole life, like a hamster spinning in a wheel going nowhere.

If you take an honest look at your to-do list, you'll notice that many tasks can be let go. For the remaining tasks, use your full focus and all your creativity to complete them as quickly as possible.

Value your 'dream list' over your 'to-do list'. Let's focus on the 'things you'd love to do', rather than the 'things you have to do'. Obligations eat away at freedom, but dreams liberate you from within.

Your inner voice is quiet. When it whispers within you, listen closely – and write down what it says before it fades. Sometimes it's easiest to hear it when you're in situations where you can't do anything else – for example, when you're in the bath or the toilet, doing yoga or swimming and so on. The voice that sleeps deep inside you can awaken and become louder when you're travelling, camping, trekking or doing something out of the ordinary, too.

Dreams can be small or vast – a movie to watch, a person to meet, a country to live in or a life's work

LET GO OF YOUR TO-DO LIST

to accomplish. Write down everything that matters to you and compile a list from it.

A dream list is a compass that guides you in designing a life true to yourself. We are born into this life to do what we truly love. We instinctively knew this when we were born. Now it's time to return to that point of origin.

●

SHIFT from
'What do I have to do?'
to
'What do I love to do?'

15

Let go of majority rule

●

SING FOR ONE

Focus on one clear vision and go all in.

'Work' isn't something that one person can complete alone. There are tasks that can't be done by yourself, and specialists are often needed. Work can only be completed when everyone communicates regularly, respects each other's situations and supports one another throughout the process.

However, simply being considerate of each other for politeness' sake is pointless.

Imagine you were having a discussion about developing a new product, and you did your best to include a little bit of everyone's opinions, because you wanted to be nice to everyone. You would probably end up with a product lacking a single standout feature. It would be a product that many people find acceptable but no one truly wants. This is why no one trusts people-pleasers who try to make everyone happy.

Majority rule is the worst. First, what is this so-called 'majority' in society? It's an illusion – just an assumption we've been taught to accept as truth. Don't do half-baked work just to earn a half-hearted 'okay' from everyone.

When your heart screams, 'This will work!', make your bold decision and stop worrying about other's reactions. Then put everything into that decision and be ready to take full responsibility. Only after that should you let your brain get involved, because your brain always blocks your decisions with so-called rational reasons.

Consider every possible scenario, thoroughly test ideas and make a detailed plan. It may lack something here or there, but it will have an outstanding and appealing feature found nowhere else.

A great product is always the fruit of someone's burning passion. A song that reaches the hearts of

LET GO OF MAJORITY RULE

a million people was written for just one person. Only these kinds of things can change the world. Every person has a project in their life they should give their everything to.

●

SHIFT from
'Needing everyone's approval'
to
'Trusting your voice'.

'Deciding what not to do is as important as deciding what to do.'

STEVE JOBS
Founder of Apple (1955–2011)

Minimalist of Simplicity
who let go of luxury in life and created radically
minimal-design products.

16

Let go of regular hours

●

GO AT YOUR OWN PACE
Don't twist yourself to fit other people's schedules.

'A good employee is someone who does more projects than everyone else, stays at the office later than everyone else and does more work than everyone else, too.' I'm sure many people's image of a good employee might sound similar to that.

There may be times when you have to stay late to make sure all the work gets done. Maybe you've even experienced working alone at the office until late at night, feeling secretly proud of yourself for working so much harder than everyone else.

LET GO

But if you really want to improve your performance at work, you should be just as conscious of cutting out as much as you can from your schedule.

Avoid filling your schedule with regular, recurring events that eat up your time for the foreseeable future. Make plans that reduce your time lost travelling from one event to the next. Leave some time and space between your scheduled items as well. Add in personal you-time that you can use however you like.

Instead of doing overtime today to finish things that could be done tomorrow, leave on time so you can prioritize your health and well-being, and do those remaining tasks first thing in the morning.

Don't adjust your schedule to always work at the same time and pace as everyone else. You could try coming into work early instead of staying late to work overtime, and ask your boss if you can take your lunch at 11.30 instead. Just by shifting your schedule away from everyone around you, the scenery of your everyday life will suddenly change.

Already too busy to control your time any further? Let's take a breath and a bit of courage: try cancelling some upcoming plans that can wait. (You don't need to explain your reasons in detail. If you ask sincerely, usually it's enough. (Even 'I want to restore my energy' is a valid reason – one I often use myself!)

Then, use the time you opened up in your schedule to have a meeting with yourself. Write down the answers to the questions 'What do I want to do right now?' and 'What do I need to do in order to achieve that?'

Obviously you won't be making progress on any work during this time. However, you'll find that once you clear your mind and go back to your tasks, your remaining work will get done at miraculous speeds and you will feel like a different person.

Don't tie yourself down to someone else's daily schedule and tasks. Making your own timetable is the door to your own freedom.

●

SHIFT from
'It's lunchtime, so I must have lunch'
to
'I'm hungry, so I'll have lunch now'.

17

Let go of your assumptions

●

NO CHANGE, NO FUTURE
It is not others, but you, who holds yourself back.

We all have rules for ourselves. 'I have to do it this way.' 'This is how I should be.' 'It must be like this.' 'I don't want to do that.' When you keep insisting on your personal rules, they eventually become part of your personal brand. However, it's a good idea to review your rules from time to time.

When you believe your rules are absolute, it becomes hard to break old patterns. Even when life, work or society shifts, you still fail to take new action to change your habits. Sometimes those rules can become a heavy burden.

Some people carry things with them for a lifetime just because they once liked them or thought they needed them. It operates as their unconscious rule. They never think to put it down, even as a trial. So they end up carrying it forever.

Whenever you notice the words 'must', 'should' or 'have to', stop for a moment. Ask yourself quietly, 'Is that really true?' 'What if it's not what I thought?' 'What if there's another way?'

It's critical to have personal rules that serve as your guiding principles. However, it's more important to rewrite those rules as you move forward.

Accept and allow yourself to be a little different than you were before. Don't be stubborn about what type of person you assume yourself to be. Sometimes you have to relax and welcome the new version of yourself.

Even if you feel uncomfortable with the new you, you can always adjust it. After all, it's a version you chose for yourself. It's far more dangerous to live a life restricted by unnecessary rules, without even realizing it. If you can love the new version of yourself, you gain another level of freedom.

LET GO OF YOUR ASSUMPTIONS

●

SHIFT from
'This is how I should be'
to
'This is how I want to be'.

18

Let go of your rational brain

LISTEN TO YOUR BODY

Believe in your intuition.

Are you scared of being rejected? If you don't trust in your own sensor – your soul – you will always be driven by other people's opinions.

If you feel something is good, it's good. If you like it, you like it. Don't trust the voice in your head. It's constantly polluted by the noise of the outside world. Your soul, however, remains untouched. Results based on calculations or research are secondary information. They lack life, and the answers they give you will always be second best and pull you away from your full potential. Answers driven by cost-benefit or profit-first thinking carry no real energy.

Physical abilities and intelligence differ from person to person, but our ability to *feel* is completely equal.

Close your eyes. Empty your head. Listen to your body — a vessel of your soul.

Your body reacts to a scent or a sound— a vague sensation, something catching your attention. The answer is hidden within those subtle feelings, and your soul already knows it.

Sometimes, it reveals itself through clear signals. Your heartbeat gets faster. Goosebumps appear on your skin. A warmth spreads through your chest. Or your body feels light, as if it's floating. To put it simply, it either feels good or it doesn't. You either like it or you don't. All you have to do to find out is access those sensations.

What touches people's hearts doesn't come from research, calculation or reason. It comes from something deeper — an invisible presence I call the soul, felt only through the body.

There's no need to explain a drive or passion that can't be put into words. Just trust it completely. And then, let it set your heart on fire and love it with all your being.

Don't get tied down by past success, industry conventions, whatever the numbers or AI say. Never make major decisions based only on logic. Use your brain not as the master, but only as the finest tool, like your hands and feet. Use it only to shape the sparks rising from your soul. That is the time to use your brain to the fullest — until it comes alive.

As long as you get this order right, your work will eventually move many people's souls.

●

SHIFT from
'What is the right answer?'
to
'What feels right to me?'

19

Let go of procrastination

●

NOW IS THE TIME
It's natural to feel hesitant or scared.

'Should I do this or not?' If you're looking for reasons to delay or excuses not to do something, you will always find them. It's also easy to find something that makes it inconvenient.

When you do something new, the moment right before you begin is always the scariest and most daunting.

'It's probably fine to put this off till later.' 'Is this really right for me?' 'Is there even any point to doing this?' The more you put things off with thoughts like these, the harder it will be to start. When a real obstacle eventually arrives — the hurdle you truly have to jump — it will feel enormous. But the most important and difficult hurdle is this very first, tiny one.

The human brain is designed to avoid risks in order to survive, and it can prevent us from taking on new challenges. That's why the first step, which demands the most courage, is more valuable than half the entire journey. As you keep clearing small, low hurdles, one after another, the time finally comes. The highest hurdle you really have to jump is right in front of you. Then you will see how all that training has paid off. There will be no hesitation or fear left, and you'll be able to take your biggest jump with all your strength.

Not taking action is what makes your life unfree. It's not being unable to do something that we should be ashamed of, but not even trying. First and foremost, you must clear your mind and take action. It's okay if you can't do it well. Of course you'll be clumsy on your first step. When you feel anxious, accept that feeling and try to clarify what you really want to do. That way, anxiety turns into a clear task you can face. You may find the task was simpler to overcome than you expected, or you may discover a clue that leads you toward a solution.

The place you are now is not everything. First, just take one step beyond it. You'll find yourself in a totally new world, with breathtaking views you've never imagined.

●

SHIFT from
'This feels too heavy, so I'll give up'
to
'I'll just start and figure things out as I go'.

20

Let go of balance

●

BE A SPECIALIST

Don't try to be good at everything.

'The main thing is to keep the main thing the main thing.' Stephen R. Covey's global bestseller *The 7 Habits of Highly Effective People* features this phrase. It shows the power of choosing one thing, making it your top priority, and giving it your full focus. A top achiever isn't someone who can handle everything smoothly. It's someone who can find something to love in the work before them. They face the work earnestly and take it on in their own way, without hesitation.

They trust that this is the one thing they have, and they carry it through to the end.

Let's think that you are one piece of a huge jigsaw

puzzle. It's good that we're all different and irregular. Our dents and bumps let us connect in a perfect fit, complementing what the other lacks. Together, we can take on great, challenging projects – and complete magnificent jigsaw puzzles.

'I'm pretty good at this, so I'll try something else.' 'I want to master this, so I'll keep going.' That choice is a turning point in your work and it shapes your life.

Life is too short to waste on fixing your weaknesses or overcoming what you're not good at. For something you're only moderately good at, ask someone better than you for help. Then you can dedicate your precious time to one thing. Pour your whole heart into the main thing you can lose yourself in forever. (Except addictive screens like video games, streaming sites and social media – designed to hijack your attention and time.)

Then, let go of everything else. Once you make that courageous decision, your life begins to shine and confidence floods through you. That's the moment you reconnect to your true self. Your inner artist awakens, but I don't mean professional artists. Anyone who focuses on one thing following their

LET GO OF BALANCE

inner voice is an artist. Those who create their own life in this way are all true artists. Indeed, we are all born artists, but we've just forgotten along the way to adulthood. I believe that my 'one thing' – my calling – is to reveal the hidden artist within you.

●

SHIFT from
'I can manage it pretty well'
to
'This is the one thing no one else can do'.

'It is not the man who has too little, but the man who craves more, that is poor.'

SENECA

Stoic philosopher (4 BCE–65 CE)

Minimalist of Inner Freedom who let go of desire and found wealth in needing little.

STEP 3

•

Health & Mindset

Many people take pride in being busy. When we get high on busyness, we tend to overestimate our own capacity. We believe we can handle an ever-increasing workload by willpower alone. But the problem is that you rarely notice when you're over capacity. To avoid becoming someone who always feels exhausted, keep a quiet intention within you. Stay true to yourself, listening carefully to your body and heart – your inner voice.

21

Let go of late nights

●

RISE AND SHINE
A well-shaped morning shapes the rest of your day.

The most important thing in life is sleep. Sleep is not the end of today, but the beginning of tomorrow. While you're sleeping, your body strengthens its immunity, clears away fatigue and removes the stress that builds up throughout the day.

However, the golden time of sleep only occurs in the first three hours after you fall asleep. During this time, growth hormone is released throughout your body, which promotes muscle and bone growth, skin repair and fat metabolization. That's why falling asleep in good condition is so important.

Spend a relaxing evening and go to bed earlier. One of the biggest enemies of good sleep is the screen – your phone, tablet, computer or TV. Blue light is the strongest visible light on Earth, and it seriously disturbs your body's sense of night and day. Never-ending information overloads your brain, and social media shakes your emotions. Put your phone away at least an hour before bed – ideally two hours – and give your mind a real break. If you can turn this into a habit, your physical exhaustion that no amount of sleep could fix will melt away.

The second most important thing is how you wake up in the morning. In big cities it can be bright as day even in the middle of the night, which can easily throw off your body's natural rhythm. But exposure to morning light releases serotonin automatically, and your body's internal clock can be reset instantly.

Immediately after you've reset, your brain goes into its active mode, and concentration and creativity levels peak. This state continues throughout the morning before starting to decline from midday into the evening. As sunlight fades away, your body releases melatonin and the brain enters rest mode. At this point, it feels like your ability to be active and energetic is instantly drained.

LET GO OF LATE NIGHTS

The fact that humans are more productive in the mornings has been true since the hunter-gatherer era. When your life follows the rhythm of the sun, your body and brain work at their best. This lifts the quality of your work, your physical health, your emotional stability — and even your 運気 (*Unki*), a Japanese concept of overall 'good fortune' in life.

If you go to bed early and fall asleep in good condition, getting at least seven hours of deep sleep, waking up early isn't a struggle. Of course, there are times in life when you cannot control your sleep — such as when caring for a baby. Even then, remembering these principles will make it easier to return to this rhythm once life has settled down.

Let yourself appreciate the quiet beauty of dawn — when the world shines at its most beautiful. Then breathe in the clean morning air and fill your lungs with fresh energy. Step outside and enjoy the morning sunlight that refreshes your body and mind.

When you reunite with the long-forgotten positive impact of mornings, you'll start to look forward to waking up.

LET GO

●

SHIFT from
'I'm not sleepy yet'
to
'I'll close my eyes when it gets dark'.

22

Let go of poor sleep

●

BE HUNGRY AND REST

Create the perfect environment for good sleep.

Going to sleep on an empty stomach is a good way to improve the quality of your sleep. It's a simple way to put your body into a state of light fasting once a day.

We call the first meal of the day 'breakfast' because we 'break' the overnight 'fast'. That's why it's best to go to bed with an empty stomach – letting your body rest in a true fasting state. For much of human history, people were unable to control the amount of food they had on hand. Humans were often forced to endure starvation for periods of time, so our bodies developed to become tougher on an empty stomach.

LET GO

Sleeping on an empty stomach allows the body to fight viruses and pathogens in the best condition possible, and it can repair the digestive organs. An empty stomach also allows you to sleep more deeply and wake up feeling more refreshed in the morning.

In the evening, a few hours before bed, it's best not to turn on all the lights. Keep the room slightly dim. Soft, indirect lighting is ideal. You can also use candles.

Eliminate 'noise' around your bed and surround yourself with only comforting items. If you can afford it, replace your cheap mattress and sheets with higher-quality ones. Your bed is where you spend a third of your life, so don't be stingy about this.

On nights when you struggle with falling asleep, turn on a relaxing radio programme or podcast at a low volume or reread your favourite collection of short stories, which you can keep by your bed. This is how I deal with insomnia.

If you still can't fall asleep no matter how hard you try, it's okay to simply close your eyes. That's enough to allow your body and mind to rest. There's no need to get upset and try to force yourself to sleep.

In short, make full use of your body throughout the day, enough to make you tired at night. Eat a light dinner early in the evening, turn the lights down as soon as you can and make your way to bed peacefully.

All you really need to do is live in harmony with the Earth, the way humans were designed to live. When your sleep quality improves, you'll recognize that your whole life and the work you do are also moving in a positive direction.

●

SHIFT from
'I'll just have a little midnight snack'
to
'I'm hungry, so I'll go to sleep'.

23

Let go of overeating

●

A HUNGRY DOG HUNTS BEST
Humans are not built to handle overeating.

People today tend to overeat. It's not because they're hungry, but because they feel bored or anxious. Often, they eat for the sake of socializing. Since our health and body shape don't collapse right away, few people actually worry about eating too much – unless we're on a diet. Let's simply decide: if you're not hungry, don't eat. Before you allow overeating to become an unconscious habit, make the conscious decision not to eat unless you're hungry. We should eat because we feel hungry, not because it's noon or 7 p.m.

However, in the long history of humankind, which spans 2.5 million years, widespread overeating has only really been around for about 100 years. It's been scientifically proven that the human body still hasn't adapted to cope with the effects of overeating.

Unlike cows, humans can't store extra food in their stomachs. Therefore, overeating not only leads to more body fat, but also weakens blood vessels and internal organs. It can cause serious damage to the human body.

The worst thing you can do is overeat before going to bed. The modern human's addiction to staying full twenty-four hours a day is the root cause of all kinds of diseases in adulthood. You might feel guilty about leaving food on the plate that was served to you, but forcing yourself to eat too much will only make your stomach feel too heavy, cause you to feel sleepy and potentially even make you sick. Some scientists have shown that being a little hungry for short periods can bring you many benefits. It helps your body repair itself and become more resilient – and it also supports long-term health.

Don't get stuck on eating three meals a day at specific times. Wait until you're hungry, then take your time enjoying the meal.

LET GO OF OVEREATING

●

SHIFT from
'I can still eat more'
to
'Do I really want to keep eating?'

24

Let go of your everyday routine

●

A LITTLE VARIETY CHANGES EVERYTHING

Try a different lifestyle today than you had yesterday.

The below is a sample day, a way of living today a little differently from yesterday, and at the same time one possible 'ideal' rhythm. Some of these small changes may already be part of your routine, while some may be new to you.

When you wake up in the morning, take in a big breath of fresh morning air. No two days are exactly alike: the colour of the sky, the chirps of the sparrows, the energy of the city starting to awaken

LET GO

or the movement of the breeze. When you focus your attention on attempting to feel the small changes happening on this planet, your five senses awaken.

As the sun rises, head to the park with a laptop or notebook in hand. Have a meeting with yourself, where you can look within while connecting with nature. You can experience the most freedom before the world starts its busy day.

Get to work earlier than anyone else, before rush hour. Eat lunch earlier, and finish the day earlier, too. Go to a new restaurant for dinner right after it opens for the evening, before it has a chance to get crowded.

Enjoy the time you spend with close friends at a different restaurant than usual, talking about a different topic than usual. Say you have an early start the next day and wrap things up at a decent hour to go home. Take a different route home than you usually do. When you get there, take a bath or a shower and change into some comfortable pyjamas. Make some tea and finish getting ready for tomorrow while listening to some good music. Then, it's lights out.

LET GO OF YOUR EVERYDAY ROUTINE

Getting into bed at an early hour is one of the most luxurious things you can do for yourself. After the sun goes down, the human brain is designed to stop functioning the way it does during the day. Thoughts have a tendency to get more negative and critical at night, so leave your worries for the next day and go to bed. And at the break of dawn, a completely new day will be there to greet you.

Try changing your everyday routines little by little. You don't need to change your whole day at once; small daily changes are what truly transform your life. What's more, even a small shift to beginning your routine a little earlier can break the negative cycle. It frees you from the feeling of being chased by time and allows every hour to become truly yours.

●

SHIFT from
'Will anything good happen today?'
to
'What can I do to make today the best day ever?'

25

Let go of the presence of others

•

BE YOURSELF

Go out into nature alone.

When I was young, I lived alone in Tokyo. Even though the city was filled with all sorts of sounds, and it was bright outside even at night, I felt constantly lonely.

I was also weighed down by an indescribable feeling of stress. When I was alone in my room, I could still feel other people's presence. That made my loneliness even worse. I realized it wasn't that I felt lonely *because no one was there*. I felt lonely *because I could sense other people* all the time.

Looking back, I'm sure there were other factors, too. My work life was full of doubt and struggle, I was too busy with socializing, and my mind was overloaded with noise. This made my thoughts more complicated, my emotions more unstable. I was worrying about things that were out of my control.

I left Tokyo for a weekend and headed to the forest by the lake, just one hour from my place. It was completely silent there; and no one was around me. All I could hear was wild birds singing and the sound of the wind rustling the leaves. Yet I didn't feel lonely at all. Even when I spent the night there alone in my van, I felt no craving to connect to someone like I felt back in the city.

Surrounded by wild nature on my weekend trips, I could finally breathe — freely and calmly. My thoughts became simple and clear. My emotions settled, and all those worries tangled up inside me just melted away. Back in my weekday life, I thought I was too busy to have this peaceful moment. But those weekends in the forest finally helped me see the truth: the issue wasn't a lack of time. It was my restless mind that kept rushing me and stopped me from finding the peace that was already there.

Spend time away from your work and everyday life, and let go of constant thinking. This is how a scattered mind resets. The environment of pure, noiseless nature has the power to bring you back to your true self.

I personally love forests and lakes, but the same is true for the beach, mountains, rivers, deserts or open wilderness — any place in nature where you hardly feel the presence of people. And if wild, untouched nature is far away from where you live, a park, a small pond or a bench in the shade of trees is more than enough. What matters most is simply placing yourself in an outdoor space where you can step away from people and constant noise. When I was in Tokyo, I sometimes escaped to the empty rooftop of my flat, where no one ever came.

When you do this, remember that above your head stretches the vast sky, and beneath your feet lies the nature of the land. Feel the scents on the wind, the shifting clouds, the blessed sunlight and the Earth that sustains all life. With gratitude, take a moment to affirm that you are alive here and now.

LET GO

●

SHIFT from
'I don't have time to go out into nature'
to
'I'll make time to go out into nature'.

'Our life is frittered away by detail ... Simplify, simplify.'

HENRY DAVID THOREAU
American writer and philosopher (1817–1862)

Minimalist of Simple Living who let go of convention to live self-sufficiently with few possessions by the lake.

26

Let go of other people's common sense

●

STAY FOOLISH

Schedule some 'art time' for yourself.

Everyone was born an original artist, because there is only one you. However, many people hesitate to admit it. Does the word sound too lofty? Maybe you believe you can't make a living that way. Or you try not to be unique because you don't want to be laughed at. The 'rational' advice of your parents, teachers or friends may have discouraged you.

The fear of being seen as different may have suppressed and locked away the artist within you.

Whether we realize it or not, each of us is drawing our own picture on the white canvas of life. No two people are the same, among eight billion on this planet. That's why each one of us is born as a one-of-a-kind artist by nature.

Make time to remember who you are. This is your 'artist time', a time to use for expressing yourself fully. Here's how to practise it: I recommend three patterns. First, for at least fifteen minutes daily – just 1 per cent of your twenty-four hours – combine simple meditation (lesson 30) and offline time (lesson 45). Second, every weekend, try a nature escape (lesson 25) or a long walk (lesson 27). Third, go on a retreat once a year – my definition of ultimate luxury is 'doing nothing in an extraordinary place'.

I'm not saying you have to start painting, writing poems or performing dance. Simply try to connect with your soul and listen to your inner voice. When stillness returns to your mind, the quiet spark naturally blossoms within you. Your long-neglected truest feelings will come back to life.

You may think artist time isn't something a normal person would do. But what we call 'being normal' is just an illusion – a meaningless belief made up by others. If you don't let go of other people's norms, you'll never reclaim your true self. Even if it's for a few moments, make time just for yourself, free from other people's judgement.

Your inner voice, the artist within you, speaks very quietly. With even the slightest noise around, you won't be able to hear it. Step away from information, crowds and distracting words. Enter a state of inner peace. Release the tension in your body, and remember who you are – just as you are. This is what heals you most deeply, and the more time you spend here, the richer your life becomes.

●

SHIFT from
'How will I be judged?'
to
'What can I create?'

27

Let go of disturbing words

●

YOU ARE WHAT YOU SAY

Walk until your words fade away.

What kind of words do you usually say to yourself?

When you get tired of everyday life, negative words flood your head. 'Why does it always happen to me?' 'I can't stand what he said.' 'So irritating!' Aggressive words bleed into you – and gradually create a rough, unsettled atmosphere around you. They disturb not only your mind but your life itself.

The scary thing about such words is that the more you use, the more your emotions heat up. The easiest way to break out of that cycle is to walk away and go somewhere else. Simply cut off what you're doing and step outside.

Take a deep breath of fresh air and look up at the sky. Begin walking slowly, observing the movement of the clouds. The clouds remind you of the wind's presence. Feel the air gently brush your cheeks. The sky is the most immediate piece of Mother Nature you can access anytime. Even in a city filled with tall buildings, look straight up and the vast sky is always there. Deep, wide, with the entire universe beyond.

Once you've calmed down a bit, try to quietly observe your emotions as you walk. Imagine you were looking down from the sky above, just gazing softly. Then, a moment comes when you naturally slip out of the 'me, me, me' mode you were stuck in.

If your mind is still unsettled, try to see how far you can walk on your next day off. The act of walking has the power to simplify your thoughts and calm your emotions. The more you walk, the more noise falls away from your mind. You'll see with greater clarity what new actions to take.

People today spend too little time walking. Walking meditation is one of the oldest forms of meditation. If you lose track of your own rhythm and no longer hear your inner voice, take a walk. When you walk long distances, you realize you're moving forward by your own strength alone. This awakens a quiet confidence within you.

Walk the Earth to reconnect with your true self through your body — to remember why you were born to this planet.

●

SHIFT from
'Why me?'
to
'What can I do?'

28

Let go of relying on sheer willpower

●

SLOW DOWN AND GO FURTHER
To reach your highest peak, enjoy the journey itself.

Many people take on lots of different tasks all at once and never give their minds a chance to rest. When you grow up and enter the workforce, quick results are always expected of you. You can easily become burdened with more work than you can handle before you even know it. Small daily strains quietly build up little by little.

If you continue to push yourself to extremes, eventually you'll get used to it, and before long that bad habit will turn into everyday life. Soon you may no longer be aware of your own stress or weariness.

No matter how much you love your work, the secret to enjoying it and performing better is to take some time to rest before you exhaust yourself.

In the world of long-distance trekking, not listening to your body can be fatal. If your breathing becomes strained or irregular, slow down or take a break. If your legs feel heavy, stop and stretch. If you sweat too much, take off a layer of clothing. In the high mountains, feeling thirsty is a sign you're already dehydrated.

If you deal with each small sign as it comes up, you can enjoy every step of the journey. Even after two weeks of trekking, you won't feel any tiredness.

I was once taught that long-distance trekking can be 修行 (*Shugyō*) – a Japanese practice of self-training. It is a traditional form of disciplined mental training. That no matter how hard the path, we must endure and push forward with our sheer willpower until we reach the peak.

These are the same values many of us absorbed as we became working adults. But times have changed. The idea that you must endure lack of sleep or exhaustion from busyness and keep pushing forward is nonsense.

Observe your body and mind every day and pay attention to even the slightest discomfort. Over the long term, this is the smartest way to protect yourself and sustain high performance. It's also the only way to walk the steep trail with joy and still reach the highest peak. In other words, it's the best strategy to achieve meaningful and truly outstanding results in your work.

If you think being a working adult means enduring heavy burdens, you'll never be able to enjoy the splendid view along the way to success.

●

SHIFT from
'How much can I endure?'
to
'How much can I enjoy?'

29

Let go of studying without a why

●

A QUALIFICATION IS JUST A TOOL
Studying that weighs down your heart is meaningless.

If you are an adult, there is nothing more useless than studying 'just in case', without any clear purpose. Not only are they useless, but they also drain your precious time, money and energy. Qualifications, certificates and what you study should be determined by whether they will help you achieve your goals or dreams. If you don't yet know what your goals and dreams are, focus on three foundations that will support you on any path.

First, build strong information-filtering skills: the

ability to spot fake news, check sources and choose reliable information. In an age of misinformation, these skills are your primary shield. Here's a story. When I worked in Tokyo, I radically limited my information sources. It kept me out of trends, but that's why I produced many hits. Because I wasn't seeing what everyone else was seeing, I could act on fresh, original ideas. The truth is — except in a crisis, we need far less information than we think we do.

Second, to achieve ultimate efficiency, completely master the latest technology, such as AI and smart appliances. Many people think of them as magic solutions, but they're only tools that amplify your own input or knowledge. You're the one who maximizes the performance of AI and smart appliances to handle chores in your work and daily life — at maximum speed. Then invest all your reclaimed free time in what only you can create or what leads to your dreams. Of course, you can use it on your 'artist time'. Never waste it on trivial tasks that don't truly matter.

Third, gain basic conversational skills in a second language. You might think AI translation makes this unnecessary, but the truth is the opposite. Its output

LET GO OF STUDYING WITHOUT A WHY

depends entirely on your ability. To get high-quality results from AI, you need your own language skill to guide it and check its accuracy. As a Japanese writer living in New Zealand for years, I still struggle to understand fast English speech. I sincerely hope this book will help not only native speakers but also non-native speakers like me – especially those struggling with modern society, as I did. Because even in an AI age, direct and passionate human words remain the heart of friendship.

If English is your native language, you can challenge yourself with another widely spoken language like Spanish or Mandarin Chinese.

It's also perfectly fine to learn a minor language simply because you love a country. That love alone is enough, even if it never helps your career. If you have a deep fascination with Japanese culture, or if you really love manga and anime, you'll master Japanese faster than anyone else. (You're more than welcome to – let's talk in Japanese someday!) No amount of effort can beat genuine passion.

Many non-native English speakers struggle to learn English, and I completely understand this as a Japanese person. But the English people use all around the world is actively changing. For example, the language used on websites and social media is becoming simpler. This is because the number of non-native speakers of English is rapidly increasing, and many people rely on simple English as a universal communication tool. If you need a higher level of English for business negotiations or tricky presentations, translation AI will support you. Therefore, a non-native speaker doesn't need to learn difficult vocabulary or grammar. If you're a native English speaker, the same truth applies when you learn any other language.

Even native English speakers would benefit from letting go of overly complex language in messages, conversations and posts online. This helps you to be better understood by people who speak different levels of English internationally. Using fancy words and phrases to sound smarter will never be as powerful. In the end, simple, honest and heartfelt words communicate best.

As a teenager, I let go of all my other subjects and focused on studying English to pursue my dream of living a life beyond Japan. Because of that choice, I was able to gain extraordinary freedom.

LET GO OF STUDYING WITHOUT A WHY

Don't fall into the trap of studying just for its own sake. Decide what you truly need to master to move toward your goals and dreams. Learn it in the most minimalist and efficient way you can – and use it to gain your true freedom.

●

SHIFT from
'Let's learn more'
to
'Let's learn what matters'.

30
Let go of the noise

●

HEAR THE SILENCE

There is no easier way to heal yourself than deep breathing.

I believe that meditation is the easiest way to bring peace back into your busy life. It settles your mind, letting you focus on what matters most.

Some people may feel hesitant about the word 'meditation', but trust me, it's quite easy. All you have to do is find a quiet place, either close your eyes or leave them half-open and focus on your breath. Think of it as a long version of deep breathing – just taken a little further. One day, when trekking in the Japanese Alps, I met a man from Nepal who showed me a simple way to do it.

First, sit cross-legged on the floor or sofa. Or sit on

LET GO

the chair you use every day. Gently close your eyes and mouth, and turn your attention to your breath. Start by breathing out completely, then breathe in deeply.

Focus only on the sound of your breath, as if you're simply following it, slowly. Fresh air passes through your nose and fills your lungs. Pay attention when you breathe out, even more than when you breathe in.

After that, allow your mind to travel from the top of your head down towards your feet as slowly as possible. Start with the feeling of your hair, then your scalp, to your skull, and inside your brain. Feel your eyebrows, eyelids, eyelashes, eyes, nose, lips, chin. Next, move your attention down the back of your throat and through each part of your body. Just once, let your mind rest at your chest and tune in to your heartbeat.

Once you reach your toes, widen your awareness. Notice the clothes you're wearing and the room you're in. Then imagine the whole building, your neighbourhood, the city, the region or state, and finally the country. Pull the camera of your consciousness outward – to your continent, to the whole world – if possible to the moon.

Start by practising this for fifteen minutes – just 1 per cent of your twenty-four hours – then aim for thirty. The longer you stay in meditation, the lighter your head and warmer your feet will feel. Not only will it clear your thoughts and quiet your emotions, but your entire body will feel refreshed as well.

One last thing: a minimal meditation you can do in just sixteen seconds. Breathe in deeply for four seconds, hold for four seconds, then slowly breathe out for eight seconds. Research from Harvard found that doing this '4–4–8 breathing' just four times activates your relaxation mode. In my experience, it works so dramatically that, even when my head is hot with anger, a single round calms me down.

Any meditation method is fine. Simply maintaining good breathing allows you to feel your soul. Once you do, you can let go of your ego and return closer to the nothingness before birth. It echoes ancient Taoist philosopher Lao Tzu's words: 'When I let go of what I am, I become what I might be.'

●

SHIFT from
'Trying not to think'
to
'Looking within yourself'.

'The secret of happiness lies in the mind's release from worldly ties.'

GAUTAMA BUDDHA
Founder of Buddhism (c. 6th–5th century BCE)
Spiritual Minimalist
who let go of royal life and all possessions to seek liberation from suffering.

STEP 4

•

Relationships

It's okay if you're not very sociable. It's okay if you can't speak fluently. You don't need many people on your side.

Instead of trying to keep up with everyone, treasure your truest friends and family who make you feel comfortable and bring out your true self. When you devote your time and energy to those relationships, you can refocus on your own life. Over time, the social pressure and heaviness you once felt in front of others will start to fade.

31

Let go of your network

●

GO OFF ROAD

Weird people find freedom because they stop getting pointless invitations.

Saying no is an act that takes a lot of energy.

Many people try to actively cultivate as many relationships as possible. They think that even in relationships without true emotional connection, it's best not to cut off communication – because you never know when you might need someone's help.

However, it's better to be dismissed as 'the antisocial one' than to keep forcing yourself to be cheerful and go along with everyone else. Spend the precious time

LET GO

you gain by stepping away from unnecessary socializing on yourself – or on those who truly matter to you. It feels terrible to receive a message and not send a reply. It's hard to ignore a phone call from someone who might need you. The more people you make connections with, the more your own time is lost. In other words, part of your life becomes someone else's property.

To start with, you don't actually need many shallow relationships in your life. All that a wide and shallow network of acquaintances will give you is the feeling of security that you know a lot of people. It will also rob you of your time. There's no point in collecting business cards – they rarely lead to anything meaningful.

It's okay if people think you're a little strange or different. When you're weird, you may feel a little lonely, but you'll be free from needing to wear a mask to fit in with everyone else. You'll feel more yourself and learn to see which people in your life truly matter.

Thanks to social media, connecting with other people like yourself is now easier than ever, regardless of physical distance. The more you share

LET GO OF YOUR NETWORK

openly about your hobbies, interests and thoughts, the easier it will be to meet friends who understand you at a deeper level.

You can usually tell if someone is as weird as you the moment you meet them. And the feeling is mutual.

If you let go of your attachment to the connections you already have, life will bring you even greater ones in return.

●

SHIFT from
'Making plans just because you're free'
to
'Making plans you wouldn't miss for anything'.

32

Let go of familiarity

●

LEAVE YOUR COMFORT ZONE
Get used to being alone.

Spending time with familiar people is fun. The feelings and sensations of good times come back instantly and it feels good to be around them. Maybe you had a blast together somewhere or worked on a project you all shed sweat and tears to finish. It's just very relaxing and peaceful to spend time with friends who you can be at ease with.

But there comes a time when you may need to let go of what's most familiar to you. It's important to see who you can talk to passionately about what you're working on and who you can't.

People who only want to talk about the past or complain about work or the world we live in tend to gradually gather into groups over time. People who are focused on the now and who are truly enjoying life no longer feel the need to remain in an old familiar group.

Strangely enough, people who focus on this very moment naturally connect with each other in a community free of constraints and form bonds that go beyond casual friendship.

Stepping away from a familiar group may bring feelings of guilt, unease or quiet sadness. How you deal with those emotions is a test of living with real freedom.

It's easy to assume that where you are now is everything or that it's the place you belong. But the Earth is huge and this world is bigger than you think. There is bound to be a place just for you that feels perfect.

●

SHIFT from
'Those were the days'
to
'Alright, let's get moving'.

33

Let go of the usual holidays

●

DISCOVER TRUE FREEDOM
It's time to get serious about how you spend your time off.

In Japan we have many national holidays. There's a week-long holiday in May, another in August, lots of three-day weekends and a long New Year's holiday. I'm sure you have some big national holidays and time off from work in your culture, too.

Most people fill their days off with plans to visit tourist spots or take vacations. Or they go to the beach, go snowboarding or in Japan people love to go to hot springs. Yet there's always a gap between your high expectations of relaxation and the pain of traffic jams, waiting in long lines and dealing with big crowds.

Is the experience really worth the money, time and effort you spend?

Try shifting your days off away from everyone else's where your workplace allows. Instead of taking Saturday and Sunday off, try taking a Friday and Saturday off or a Sunday and Monday off every week or every two weeks. You could also add a paid day off to create a three-day weekend once a month.

Once a year, aim for a longer stretch of rest. Use your paid time off to take a full Monday to Friday off, and turn it into your own nine-day holiday by adding weekends before and after. When I suggested this in Japan, many readers immediately said, 'That's impossible'. Back when I worked at a music company, I took a nine-day holiday or more every year. My bosses and colleagues always criticized me for it – even though I never broke any rules about paid leave. Even so, I honestly believe the reason I became a hitmaker was that I rested more than anyone else.

In Japan, the country of workaholics, even nine days in a row can be very difficult to secure, while in many Western countries people can often take two weeks or more. Whatever your situation, push as far as possible. The key is to step away from peak holiday seasons. When you avoid the most crowded places and most expensive times, the same amount of money and time can give you a far deeper and richer experience. Even your hometown will shine as brightly as the scenery of gorgeous tourist locations.

Treat planning this longer holiday as a year-long project. Study your schedule from the past few years, and find the times of year when you have less work. These are the periods when a long break is most realistic. Then, based on that pattern, book your own holiday into next year's calendar, and quietly vow to yourself that you will protect those days just for you and your family.

Remember that the vow to yourself should always be a top priority. If work comes up, immediately reply, 'I'm sorry, I already have plans on that date.' The key is to give an immediate, polite response. It will be more difficult to refuse if you hesitate or say you need some time to think it over. Being firm in your stance will let the other person understand that you have something important going on that you can't miss. If you can do this over and over each time something comes up, you will secure and protect your own longer holiday.

If you work in a company or country where it's hard to take time off – or if you're a freelancer who feels afraid to rest – think of this as a small life hack for protecting your time and gaining your freedom. The time that you make for yourself, how you spend it and who you spend it with determine who you are.

●

SHIFT from
'What should I do on my day off?'
to
'I really want to do this, so I'm taking time off'.

34

Let go of hiding your true self

●

UNLOCK YOUR HEART

Always be the first to open up.

I used to have an abnormally strong blush, and I would get extremely nervous when meeting people for the first time. But at some point I learned that, even if it feels scary, life begins the moment you open up to people first.

I was in my late twenties, working in sales at Sony Music, when I first heard the voice of a debut soul singer. The moment his voice reached me, something deep inside began to tremble — it was so intense I almost lost all sense of my body.

Later, when I tried to promote his new release

to the stores, I wanted so badly to share that feeling. The words wouldn't come, but I couldn't stop talking. The emotion itself had taken over my voice. My face was burning hot, and my words were awkward – but I just kept saying, 'He's amazing!' over and over again. And then, all at once, I let go of self-consciousness and shame.

After a while, I realized my fear of talking to people had faded a little. If you want to know something, ask someone to teach you. If you like someone, put your feelings into words. A lot of people may find this challenging at first, as I did. Even if it's just a little at a time, make time to show your true self – slowly and honestly.

What is the difference between humans and other apes? Cultural anthropology offers a few theories about the use of fire or speech. But the theory I love is that we started singing solely for joy and emotional expression before we spoke to communicate. It's said that singing is what made us human.

When something exploded in our hearts, we had no choice but to express that emotion. If there was a water shortage, we would cry out toward the sky asking for rain. We could not stop ourselves from

LET GO OF HIDING YOUR TRUE SELF

expressing love for someone we cared about. We felt so good that we started to sing, and the joy of it carried us on. Eventually, we began to add rhythm and melody to our emotions. This is how the first songs were born. That's what I believe.

All the top artists I produced had one thing in common: the courage to bare their souls, with no hesitation at all. Even the most talented artists have flaws and weaknesses, but the moment they stand on a stage, they can bare it all and sing in the moment – in my words, 'They become pure song'.

What reaches the hearts of 10,000 people in the audience is not singing ability or a perfect voice. It is an unstoppable drive to let your true feeling fly free – with pure, honest passion.

●

SHIFT from
'I worry what people will think'
to
'I'm going to express myself freely'.

35

Let go of pleasing everyone

●

TREASURE YOUR SOULMATES

Decide who is most important to you.

We spend our lives interacting with so many people. Some we see every day, some we see regularly, some we only connect with online and some we haven't seen in a long time.

From now and for the rest of your life, who should you value most in order to live as freely as you possibly can? The answer is simple: those who took a risk for you.

These are the people who generously gave their time and effort to you without hesitation, even though they had no idea if you'd turn out to be useful somehow or if they had something to gain from you. In Japan, from ancient times until today, people like that have been called 恩人 (*Onjin*), which means saviours: those to whom we owe a debt of gratitude.

It's okay to treasure those people forever. Don't worry if other people criticize you for it. When the people who were there for you are in an emergency, pour all the time and effort you have into helping them.

There's no need to bother with people who would only talk to you if they could get something out of it. They will be there when you're in a good mood, but when you really need their help they will scramble away as fast as they can run.

There's no need to hesitate to give back to someone who was there for you. Treasure only the friends who believe in you and support you, even when there's no guarantee you'll succeed.

LET GO OF PLEASING EVERYONE

●

SHIFT from
'Let's call everyone'
to
'Let's call the person I love most'.

'Freedom is independence from the compulsory will of another.'

IMMANUEL KANT
German philosopher (1724–1804)

Minimalist of Discipline
who let go of desire to live by self-imposed order and moral freedom.

36

Let go of resisting tradition

●

NO MANNERS, NO FREEDOM
Make full use of the wisdom that came before you.

Greet people in the mornings. Say thank you sincerely when someone does something for you. If you're running late for an appointment, let them know in advance. Offer the better seat in a taxi to the most senior person in your group. Be polite when you meet someone for the first time.

When I was young and knew little about social norms, I had to learn basic manners and etiquette the hard way – getting scolded by senior colleagues. It's never too soon to master proper business etiquette. Some of them might seem ridiculous or silly. But if you continue to disregard it, you may make others uncomfortable. You might not even notice when you do it, but it will come back to bite you later. Lacking proper manners often leads to cold, harsh treatment from others – that's just how the ecosystem of human society works. No matter how good you are at your job or how charming your personality, a single act of perceived rudeness can really hurt your reputation.

If you think adults who stick to old-fashioned manners are not free, you'd be wrong. True manners are not about rules or discipline. They are about empathy – imagining how others feel and acting with respect and consideration. Once you've mastered the 型 (*Kata*) of genuine manners, life becomes much easier. *Kata* is the Japanese art of ritual templates: practising the fundamentals repeatedly until they become part of you. In judo, you practise *Kata* consistently so you don't get nervous or hurt, and can move smoothly in real matches. Then you can focus on your opponent in the match. In your life, it frees you from overthinking relationships, which drain your attention, and lets you focus on what matters most. It's not about rigid rules, but about finding freedom through simplicity.

Kata will serve as your strongest shield, protecting you for the rest of your life. People who truly live freely have mastered the *Kata* of manners – they know how to move through the world with grace.

I'm not saying to blindly follow so-called common-sense rules that have only been around for a decade. But the *Kata* of etiquette and manners – the timeless form refined through generations in every culture – carries the wisdom of our ancestors. It holds the key to avoiding strained relationships and even guides you to move through the world without friction or conflict. It is beautiful and makes total sense. No matter when you learn it, it's never too early and never too late.

●

SHIFT from
'It's such a hassle'
to
'Once I master it, I'll be free'.

37

Let go of checking messages

●

SHUT YOURSELF OFF
Disconnect from chats and phone calls as much as possible.

So many people spend a lot of time checking messages. Whether in a meeting or working, people keep their email and chat windows open all the time. What's more, unwanted messages never stop coming.

　Information that you don't want is all noise. If you respond to every single thing that comes your way, your concentration will be constantly interrupted and eventually you'll forget what you really wanted to do in the first place.

First, unsubscribe from all newsletter-type emails that have been adding up without you really noticing. You can also change your email address or chat application profile to reset yourself with a new account. But this time, think long and hard about what kind of information you really want to receive by being honest with yourself.

In addition, decide when you want to check your messages – in most cases, just mornings and evenings are fine – and mute notifications where possible. Instead of checking your messages all day, replying immediately and being distracted by notifications, take the initiative to respond only when it's your scheduled time.

Chat applications in particular can really distract your concentration and potentially mess up your life. Phone calls are dangerous, too. It's like letting people break in and stomp around your house with their dirty feet. If you answer every call that comes in, you'll lose the chance to truly be present with what matters – and with the people who matter.

When your phone rings, always ask yourself if it's a call you should answer now. Just because it's a friend, colleague or client doesn't mean you have to

LET GO OF CHECKING MESSAGES

respond immediately. Right?

Completely let go of your passive attitude about incoming information and communication. You do not need to be constantly connected to phone calls and messages twenty-four hours a day. The most important thing is always what's right in front of you.

●

SHIFT from
'Please contact me'
to
'I'll contact you'.

38

Let go of being competitive

●

CHASE NOBODY BUT YOURSELF

You don't need a rival to beat to motivate you.

Regardless of your age, occupation or status, everyone has a natural desire for recognition and approval. But it's uncool to exaggerate yourself or belittle others to try to get people to like you more.

If you don't want to lose, simply don't try to win. When you are constantly concerned about winning and losing, you tend to assume you have lost. If you keep that up, you'll develop a loser mentality.

Don't obsess over whether you're better than your friend, what rank you are in your group or how to catch up when you fall behind your rival. These days, it's also easy to compare yourself with people who are not around you – someone in another city, another country, another social class, or even strangers on your screen, whose lifestyle, career or possessions look far better than yours. Social media makes this comparison game worse and worse. But the trap is the same: the more you stare at others' lives, the more you lose sight of your own life and confidence in yourself.

The grass is not greener on the other side. Focus only on your own territory.

Don't move somewhere expensive and buy nice clothes just to impress other people. It's far better to create a space where you feel comfortable, wear clothes that put you at ease, listen to music that lifts your mood and focus fully on what you love. As long as you aren't worrying about what others think and just keep moving in the direction you truly wish to go, winning and losing don't matter at all.

In life, the person who aims for their own fulfilment is unbeatable. You should always aim for your personal best, not to be a 'winner'.

Don't look around. Look at yourself. If you continue to do things you find joyful and give yourself the

LET GO OF BEING COMPETITIVE

recognition and approval you need, wonderful people will naturally gravitate to your side.

●

SHIFT from
'I've got to beat that guy'
to
'I'm going to have fun my own way'.

39

Let go of hiding behind 'sorry'

●

EVERYONE MAKES MISTAKES
Don't try to immediately defend yourself.

It's not weak to apologize. Truly big-hearted people can face their mistakes and apologize sincerely. But if 'sorry' becomes a shield you hide behind, it stops you opening a doorway to a better version of yourself.

It's easy to admit everything is your fault. You can be forgiven for a lot of things if you simply look someone in the eye and say sorry – like being five minutes late to a meeting, making a mistake when filling out a form or overlooking a number on an order receipt.

LET GO

But if you apologize too instantly and too much, your brain stops thinking. The soul from your words is lost, which damages the trust of those around you. Not only that, but you lose faith in yourself, too.

Everyone makes mistakes. If you think you've really done something wrong, you'd better apologize sooner rather than later. The problem is when people use a simple 'sorry' to cover things up, without really dealing with the issue. If you think saying sorry is enough to make everything okay, that mindset is something you need to let go of right away. Apology should reflect accountability.

Don't be too quick to say sorry. That doesn't mean you can make excuses and slip away. It means asking yourself a few honest questions: 'Did I mess up?' 'Could my careless decision have caused this problem?' 'What exactly do I need to apologize for?'

Be clear with yourself before you bow your head. Face the cause of your mistake, reflect honestly and speak a sincere 'sorry'. Only then can you learn from failure and move forward. Only people who can keep doing that are trusted, and given better opportunities over time.

LET GO OF HIDING BEHIND 'SORRY'

●

SHIFT from
'Using an apology to avoid getting scolded'
to
'Apologizing meaningfully and mindfully'.

40

Let go of holding yourself back

●

SAY WHAT YOU THINK
When you see the right moment come,
don't miss it.

'Getting along' at work doesn't mean trying to be liked by all. When professionals are serious about their work, it's natural that there will be differences of opinion.

When overwhelmed by invisible tension, you might feel it's not your place to speak up – and quietly step back. Saying, 'I respect everyone's opinion' may sound graceful, but it could just be your way of holding back. It's easy to keep saying nice things just to maintain a peaceful atmosphere.

LET GO

However, if you only adjust yourself to others' opinions, you'll never own the work you do.

When it comes to work, there's no right answer. You may have less experience than others. But, if your inner voice says something feels off, don't be too shy to speak up. Say what you feel. Even if it ruins the mood, you should say something.

Your comment might step on someone's toes and create a tense and heavy atmosphere. You might realize it was your mistake — and be harshly criticized for it. But your words and expression can show how serious you are about your work.

True professionals don't hesitate for fear of ruining the mood. They are sincere about sharing what they really think, even if they face some push back over it more than once.

It doesn't matter how clumsy you think your words might be when you open your mouth. If you're serious, speak up.

LET GO OF HOLDING YOURSELF BACK

SHIFT from
'It's embarrassing to make mistakes'
to
'Every mistake helps you grow'.

'The less we need,
the less trouble
we can have.'

LEO TOLSTOY
Russian writer (1828–1910)

Minimalist of Truth who let go of fame to live as a humble farmer and seek moral clarity in daily life.

STEP 5

•

Lifestyle

Among the countless things you could do, there is only one thing you should do in this very moment. What do you want to do? What would bring you joy and happiness? No one can answer this for you. Listen closely to your heart. Uncover your deepest needs. Once your top priority is clear, take your first step and just do it.

41

Let go of the fear of lacking

●

BE NAKED AND GO LIGHT
Less is beautiful.

Countless traps are set in a capitalist society, making us feel anxious unless we own more than we actually need. For example, we stuff our bags with all kinds of things, just in case — books and documents, all kinds of devices, extra pens and notebooks, spare cosmetics. We even carry things we've long forgotten how and when we got them. As long as we have enough physical strength, we can somehow carry them all. In my twenties, I carried far more than I needed. Back then, I couldn't understand why I ended up exhausted every single day.

It's just like trekking. When I was younger, my backpack was overloaded and too heavy, and all I could think about was reaching the summit – I missed the joy of the journey and the beauty along the way.

But at some point, I turned my attention towards things I could do without, rather than things that might be useful. Carrying too much can lead to injuries on the mountain path. So I identified what I truly needed and kept refining my load, aiming to make it as light and minimal as possible.

In the summer before my fiftieth birthday, I took a two-week trek across the Northern Alps in Japan, the longest mountain range in the country, and my backpack weighed less than 15 kilos, yet it held everything I needed, including food, a tent, my sleeping bag and extra clothes. It was half the weight of what I carried around in my twenties, which was closer to 30 kilos.

Technological advances were one reason my gear became lighter. But what truly made the difference was experience and training. Over time, they sharpened my senses and helped me see clearly what I needed – and what I could let go of.

LET GO OF THE FEAR OF LACKING

Eventually I took this attitude beyond backpacking and into my city life as well. I began to challenge myself to see how minimal and lightweight I could keep my bags and luggage. After that, the struggle of daily life suddenly eased, and my senses grew sharper – I began to notice both the quiet details and the truly important things.

The lighter your bags, the better. This is a fact. I chose to prioritize the freedom of walking around practically empty-handed over the feeling of security you get at the cost of carrying everything around with you.

●

SHIFT from
'I should bring this just in case'
to
'I think I'll leave this at home'.

42

Let go of staying in one place

●

GO TO WHERE LIFE IS
The more you relocate your base, the more creative you become.

For most people, home is one fixed place – and so is work. We stay rooted in the same kind of location. Why? Convenience. Proximity to the station, the office, the daily commute. But should convenience alone decide where you live?

Where you live, where you work, where you spend your time – change just these, and a new way of life begins with surprising ease. You start to see what you couldn't before, meet people you never would have crossed paths with and discover values you never knew existed.

Until recently, the ability to move around and choose your lifestyle freely was limited to a privileged group of people. But with technology advancing and the global shift brought by COVID-19, living and working wherever you choose is no longer out of reach.

You can move somewhere else anytime you want to. You can try living in a city just because you're curious about what it would be like. We're finally in an age where this is possible and easy to accomplish. Forget the outdated idea of dragging everyone into the same meeting room. Why not let each person share their best ideas from wherever they feel most inspired?.

Each time you move to a new place, you have a chance to reset your life — not just your surroundings, but your mindset and belief as well. You can let go not only of old habits and fixed patterns of thought, but also of the things you own — and even certain relationships. As distractions clear away, you feel lighter and freer. Focus sharpens, energy returns and your judgement improves — setting you into a positive spiral of clarity.

LET GO OF STAYING IN ONE PLACE

Now, spread out a map and mark every spot that speaks to you (that's how I found the lake I call home). A whole new lifestyle, free from being tied to any workplace or location, is within your reach – as long as you have the curiosity to try and the belief to make it real. This truth is universal. Let it stay with you.

●

SHIFT from
'A place of convenience'
to
'A place that sparks joy'.

43

Let go of trying to choose everything

●

STAY TRUE TO YOURSELF

The more you chase, the less you can move.

What you choose to prioritize determines the quality of your life. What kind of life do you want? What is the dream you want to live for? And what should you be doing right now to make it real? What should you let go of to focus on that dream? Then, face the one clear decision it reveals – and commit to it fully.

The more you throw yourself at everything, the more unnecessary options and confusion you create. You lose sight of what matters now and end up wasting your life on things that don't matter to your dream. Those non-essential things quietly steal your time, money and energy – until suddenly, it's all gone. I listened to the quiet inner voice – the one that said, 'I want to live by a beautiful lake in New Zealand.' I let go of everything else and focused only on actions that would lead me closer to that life. That's why I was able to make clear decisions – both in daily life and at major turning points.

It did take me fifteen years, but I was able to manifest my dream because I kept my focus on the one thing I wanted. Now I fish in the lake in front of my home in New Zealand and in the nearby ocean. I forage in the forests that surround my home, and I grow organic vegetables and fruit in my own garden. When I show people pictures of my life there and the miraculous colours of the morning sunrise, they always say, 'I'm so jealous!' But many of them still believe this kind of lifestyle is impossible for them.

The lifestyle that's ideal for me might be torture for someone else – and that's okay. I don't care what other people think. The most important thing is to fully pursue the life your heart truly longs for.

Peer pressure, social standards, temptations and fleeting desires are all just noise. How do you really want to live your own life? You

LET GO OF TRYING TO CHOOSE EVERYTHING

will not find that answer anywhere except inside yourself. Listen to your inner voice. And today, decide to have the courage to follow that voice.

●

SHIFT from
'I want to do everything'
to
'I choose to do only this'.

44

Let go of the fear of being foolish

●

DECLARE YOURSELF
Let your dream speak out.

Share your true passion – the one that quietly rises from your soul – without holding back. Tell people, even strangers or through social media. Let the world know what truly matters to you.

Let go of that guarded, hesitant part of yourself. Stand tall with quiet confidence and say clearly: 'This is what I love.' Some people might roll their eyes and wonder, 'Why are you getting so passionate about this? Cool down!'

Even so, keep speaking your dream to the world. One day, you will notice some big changes.

First, the way people introduce you will be different. When I was younger, people didn't introduce me as 'Daisuke from the sales department'. They introduced me as 'Daisuke, this strange kid who always talks about his dream of moving to New Zealand'. People always reacted with bitter smiles.

It's okay. Let them laugh at you. This kind of impactful 'tagline' or 'label' helps others remember you more easily – and that alone is an advantage at work. In addition, helpful information begins to flow to you – 'There's an event coming up related to that' or 'I can introduce you to my friend who knows more about it'. If I hadn't kept saying that I wanted to move to New Zealand, no one would've come to me saying things like 'There's a special on New Zealand on TV' or 'My cousin just moved there'.

If you can plant your dream in the minds of many, they'll naturally become your supporters, helping you make it happen. Simply by clarifying your innermost longings – with pure honesty – it begins to flow to you naturally. The truth is, human society works through these kinds of beautiful ecosystems – that is one part of the greater law of circulation that governs the natural world. You don't need to worry

LET GO OF THE FEAR OF BEING FOOLISH

about the results right now – just start speaking your truth. From there, your world will quietly begin to shift.

●

SHIFT from
'I'm too shy to say what I love'
to
'This is what I love most'.

45

Let go of always being online

●

STICK TO YOUR INNER QUEST
Set aside time to go offline once a day.

High-performance devices, countless social media platforms, wide mobile networks and satellite internet. Thanks to these technologies, we can now stay connected from anywhere in the world, even deep in nature or out on the ocean. Yet that noisy feeling of being online – connected to so many people 24/7 – never goes away. Being able to contact anyone anywhere seems like the essence of a fulfilled life, but is that really true?

In this hyper-connected world, information never stops. Let yourself have offline time each day

— simply to protect your inner peace and stay true to yourself. Even in the middle of a busy day, at the very least, gift yourself fifteen minutes — only 1 per cent of your day — to disconnect completely.

Once a day, stay offline and allow your mind to rest in quiet stillness, untouched by the flood of outside information or others. Set an alarm to remind you of this moment. When it goes off, let go of your tasks and worries. Turn off Wi-Fi and mobile data — or power down completely.

Step away from your screen and release your mind from 'standby mode'. Let your body relax.

Tune your awareness only to your inner self — your breath, your body and the quiet presence of your soul. Let yourself feel: you are only here right now, in this peaceful moment, within the infinite flow of time.

You will finally begin to hear the tiny inner voice that has been drowned out by noise all day.

Breakthrough ideas may arise — ones that never came while you were scrolling online.

You may notice a slight discomfort or realize there's something you've been wanting to let go. You might also remember something you once truly loved to do that you quietly left behind.

To design your life of freedom, without being swept along by others and information, you need this time alone. This sacred time of solitude and stillness is a gift — one that allows you to reconnect with yourself.

●

SHIFT from
'Being always connected'
to
'Being connected when you choose to be'.

'In this absurd world,
where everyone wants to
consume more,
we should ask what lies
behind consumption.'

JACQUES ATTALI
French economist (born 1943)

Minimalist of Restraint
who let go of the myth of endless growth and
warned of its dangers.

46

Let go of the idea that you must never run away

●

ESCAPE IS POSITIVE
There is always another path

Courage is not required to take on a big challenge. All you need is an escape route, and make sure it's a positive one.

Back when I worked at two major music companies in Tokyo, I kept my my spirit of freedom and independence because I was always ready to walk away. I knew I had other skills. I knew I could live another way. In other words, I had plenty of escape routes.

I had fishing and camping skills, experience of farmwork, and I knew about two free campsites by the water. I lived in my tent and got food by fishing and helping local farmers in exchange for food – I'd done it as a student. I also had a teaching licence from when I once dreamed of being a teacher, and could try to move to New Zealand, which I'd longed for.

Knowing what I know now, living in a tent for years would have been very hard, and it isn't easy to be a teacher or move to New Zealand. I had no proof that everything would work out.

But that was okay. I knew that, if necessary, I had other options. Merely imagining this made me feel free and allowed me to make bold decisions in both my career and my life.

When my mind was trapped by the thought, 'This is my only option,' a frightening sense of suffocation struck me. I almost lost hope in my life.

Some believe that having an escape route is weak and that high performance only comes when there is no way out. But for me, it was always the inner assurance of having another path that gave me strength.

LET GO OF THE IDEA THAT YOU MUST NEVER RUN AWAY

Because I knew there was always a positive escape route – a path I could turn to – I didn't fear failure. I could take bold steps forward at any time. Even when I was backpacking through the mountains, I always made sure to plan an escape route in advance. That's what allows me to enjoy every great adventure with peace of mind.

Thanks to that mindset, I have achieved my dreams and lasting success and I'm proud of myself. Above all, my greatest reward was that I never regretted any key decision I made along the way.

●

SHIFT from
'Feel the fear and do it anyway'
to
'There's nothing to fear, just do it'.

47

Let go of company loyalty

●

WORK IS SOMETHING YOU CREATE
Secure several lifelines.

Suppose you're in charge of sales and you only have one client. You have no choice but to cling to them for survival. You often end up just following their demands, and you become afraid to suggest new and creative pitches or ideas.

Yet many people try to live that way, and the one single client they rely on for survival is called 'the company they work for'. It's an extremely high-risk, highly restricted environment. It's always better to have other lifelines. Even if your place of work doesn't allow side jobs, try to negotiate.

LET GO

This is how you can nourish your imagination, build experience and train your mind to see that it's completely possible for you to do other jobs and work somewhere else. This is another strategy I used when I worked for a company in my earlier days.

It's very important to have an inner safety net that reminds you there are always other paths you can take. It doesn't even have to be practical or to earn money. For me, fly fishing was a great example of this. These days, many people turn their serious hobbies into careers. I started out as just a fly-fishing enthusiast – and before I knew it, I was working professionally in the fishing industry.

Minimalist living isn't about owning nothing. It's about letting go of what doesn't really matter to you so you can focus on what you truly love, even if it looks strange or useless to others. For me, that was stacks of fly-fishing gear catalogues. To others they were just junk, but I lost myself for hours studying those hidden treasures – specs and details of all the gear. I committed to maximizing my world of fly-fishing and to minimizing almost everything else. This, too, is a core philosophy of minimalist

LET GO OF COMPANY LOYALTY

living. About ten years later, this so-called junk turned into a goldmine of ideas for designing fly-fishing and outdoor products – and brought me an income. When you become a master of what you love, you can turn that knowledge into a job teaching it to others. My pure passion for music and branding artists eventually led me to become a lecturer at a university. As I continued to develop my own unique lifestyle, offers for writing, speaking and interviews kept coming my way.

Why not try sharing what you love on social media or in a blog, and with the people you meet? It's not just me. I'm sure there are people around you who are also building up their work and careers in this way.

What matters is not doing things halfway, but falling in love with one thing completely – then going deep and mastering it. Express it freely and don't hold back. Today, people who are masters of what they love and live unconventional lifestyles are increasingly valued. Finally, geeks and oddballs like me can work freely. Work is not something you receive, it's something you create.

LET GO

●

SHIFT from
'How can I be useful to my company?'
to
'How can I be useful to the world?'

4 8

Let go of giving up

●

GO FOR IT

Fulfil your smaller wishes.

What you truly seek is not out there. It has always been within you. To find it, reconnect with the essence of who you are — as if returning to the radiant moment of your birth.

What did you like most as a child? What brought you joy or peace in those days? Try to remember those inner pulls that once moved you. Then, no matter how trivial or silly, take action. If there's something you feel called to try, do it immediately. Let your heart decide — not your head. It can be anything. If your favourite author comes to mind, buy their books and read them all. If it's the sunset you loved, go to a west-facing place and watch it until the light completely fades. When you fulfil a small wish, it leads you to another. Follow a small curiosity, and the next one will appear. Little by little, you become aware of your inner calling – the life dream that unconsciously lives within you.

In truth, we are more likely to forget our dreams than to consciously give them up. Giving up is still preferable, because at least it is your choice. But forgetting? That's the worst.

As we fall into a daily routine and life becomes more stable, it becomes easier to settle for 'this might be okay'. This kind of noise makes us forget our dreams. That's why you need a simple system in everyday life to remember them.

Start with what you see every day. Hang a picture in your living room that reminds you of your dream. In your bedroom, pin a large map of the place connected to your dream on the wall. Set the wallpaper on your phone and computer to an image that symbolizes it.

Then surround yourself with information and sounds that point you back to it. Put books that will help you achieve your dream in the centre of your bookshelf. Line your work desk with postcards that link back to your dream. Create a playlist of songs that give life to your dream.

These are the very things I kept doing for more than fifteen years. In the end, they helped me make my dream of moving to New Zealand come true.

If you can avoid forgetting your dream and keep your motivation alive, your dreams will be drawn to you naturally, no matter how big they are. It happened to me, and you will hear the same story from anyone who has brought a dream to life. If you keep remembering it and moving towards it, I promise you it will come true.

●

SHIFT from
'It would be nice if I could do that'
to
'I'll never forget what I dream of'.

49

Let go of the illusion of freedom

●

START WHERE YOU ARE
Get small results first, then aim for the next goal.

You have a big dream. You feel you shouldn't waste your time on work you don't want to do. But quitting your job without any preparation will likely cause you regret. Only then do you realize what a blessing it was to have all the facilities, proper equipment and supportive coworkers around you.

Getting fed up and suddenly quitting is like running a full marathon with zero preparation. You can try, but you're going to collapse before you reach the finish line.

LET GO

You can start training now, even as you go about completing the daily work you currently do. It's just like backpacking through the mountains for days. If you rush with big strides, you'll wear yourself out by noon. But if you stay true to your own pace and take small, steady steps, you can go much farther. Without exhaustion. With ease. Even with joy. If you feel like quitting your job, let go of all unnecessary social ties and overspending first – before making any big decisions. Let's practise minimalist living. Try to live with less and see how low you can make your living costs.

And wherever you are now, focus on building basic manners and essential work skills that will serve you wherever you go. You can think of it like being paid to learn. The boring tasks turn into lessons, and your unpleasant boss starts to look like an instructor.

Then, meet people who are active in the field you want to explore. Listen and talk to them openly, and sometimes try briefly presenting yourself. Through these small steps, you gradually clarify your direction.

But don't rush. Start where you are now. One small achievement is enough – just make something work where you stand. Quitting because things didn't

LET GO OF THE ILLUSION OF FREEDOM

work out leaves you feeling defeated. If you keep jumping from job to job without results, you'll never be fulfilled and never gain true freedom.

●

SHIFT from
'I can't do anything at this company'
to
'What can I do at this company?'

50

Let go of past success

●

RETURN TO ZERO

Instead of repeating old habits, begin again from nothing.

Fly fishing is my lifelong passion. I especially love fly fishing on the lake. The open sky, the crystal water and the purest air — I feel completely renewed. The deep green of the forest around the lake purifies not only my eyes, but my soul as well.

The wild trout carries no excess — no ornament, no waste. Their faces show no weakness or greed — only a still, razor-sharp awareness of life. Their fins are taut like blades, their scales sparkle, their streamlined bodies perfectly designed. They are the epitome of minimalist beauty.

The best part is that you can't catch them right away. You have to study what they feed on and craft flies that imitate insects and baitfish. You cast them in quiet hope, but your efforts often go ignored. You then start researching and investigating the reasons why. Through endless trial and error, all the mental noise — impure motives and hidden greed — gradually fade away. In that timeless moment, you are beyond a big ego. It is a state of true self, where all *Kegare* — the impurities that accumulate throughout a life — have been washed away.

And only then does the real breakthrough come — at last, you catch the one you've been dreaming of. In that silence, you feel a sense of oneness with nature. It is like the Zen realm of selflessness where your soul rests in truest freedom. To me, that is the supreme bliss — far beyond what we call happiness.

Yet the next day, you may use the exact same fly and technique but for some reason it doesn't work at all. Free yourself from yesterday and focus on the now. Stop chasing the trout, simply sit and observe the water.

Just like the natural world, society, the market and

LET GO OF PAST SUCCESS

your life are beyond your control.

If you rely only on calculation or theory – from your overthinking head – the best you can expect is average results.

The arrogance of thinking, 'I can win again, just like before' is quietly sniffed out. Even the smallest trace of ego is instantly sensed – by wild fish, the market and your audience or customers. Life and fishing share a simple truth. Holding on to past experiences or successes is just useless. So let them go – and your pride as well.

Always stay humble. When faced with something greater, all you can do is surrender. Let go of your ego, and accept your own nothingness. This awareness brings you back to the Zen spirit of 初心 (*Shoshin*) – 'the beginner's mind' – at any moment. Then you can embrace change without fear and keep challenging yourself throughout life.

Eventually, you'll encounter a wild fish of the most breathtaking beauty you've ever seen – like a living dream. Life works the same way. When you let go of all attachments and desires, your mind becomes completely still and free – that's when miracles happen.

LET GO

●

SHIFT from
'Trusting yesterday's catch'
to
'Listening to today's water'

'Earth provides enough to satisfy every man's needs, but not every man's greed.'

MAHATMA GANDHI
Political leader (1869–1948)

Minimalist of Non-violence
who let go of possessions and comfort to live in
simple truth.

Epilogue

Looking back, my younger years were pretty awful. All throughout my childhood, and even into adulthood, speaking in front of others always terrified me. I feared others' eyes on my blushing face, couldn't keep conversations going and was hopeless at socializing at parties. Yet I was an employee at two major music companies for years. Excessive stress caused me to break out in hives and develop facial numbness. I broke my back teeth from clenching my jaw too hard, and I fumbled even simple words like 'good morning'. When my condition was at its worst, I once passed out on the subway platform.

    They say that everyone suffers trying to be a successful adult. True freedom doesn't exist for functional members of society. Everyone is too busy just trying to make a living. These are things I told myself too, and I tried to work hard within the system. But my soul was screaming that something was very wrong.

Is becoming an adult about following others' rules, lying to ourselves and enduring it to fit in? Is that really the way it must be? I had to get out of there. That was all I could think about. Ever since my student days, I had held a specific dream in my heart: to live by a beautiful lake, in harmony with nature. I was always picturing myself at the water's edge, fly-fishing all day, every day. I would stand on the dock that extended past my garden over the lake, look down and see a large trout swimming through the pure water. Taking deep breaths, watching clouds drift by. At sunset, I see the twin screens of the sky and the lake turn brilliant scarlet.

The pure music and artists I worked with saved me too. I fell in love with producing music with artists and delivering it to listeners who needed it. For over ten years, I lost myself completely in that work. Before I knew it, I was being called a hitmaker and earning a high income.

Yet I kept my minimalist life throughout my corporate years. My peers bought luxury cars. But I cherished my old beat-up van until it was beyond

EPILOGUE

repair. It took me deep into nature to heal, where I spent countless nights sheltered inside. While others moved to expensive apartments, I stayed in a run-down flat with a graveyard on its grounds – no wonder the rent was dirt cheap. I cut all my wasteful spending, wore second-hand clothes and brought my own lunch and a reusable water bottle to keep expenses as low as possible.

Why?

For three reasons: to work in freedom, protect my true self and bring my most important dream to life.

'I have a dream to live on the lakeside in New Zealand.' Every time I told anyone this – not only personally but also at work – they gave me an awkward look. But I was serious. A job and a company are just vehicles to carry you towards your dream. As long as you know where you're going and how to drive them, any vehicle will take you there.

I knew my destination was New Zealand, so I only bought the minimum of second-hand furniture and appliances. When I finally moved, I had nothing to ship.

Yet when I cleaned out the room I'd lived in for years, preparing to leave, I still found a lot of useless

LET GO

items. I was shocked to realize how much stuff I had accumulated. This happened, even though I had no interest in brand-name products or any desire to acquire material things. Letting go of all those items I had collected in my life gave me a deep sense of liberation. It felt as if I were clearing a new path through thick dark bushes.

I set out on my journey to New Zealand without a car or a place to live, carrying only three pieces of luggage: a large backpack with outdoor wear, my MacBook and a few daily necessities; a suitcase packed with fly-fishing and camping gear; and a bulky case full of fly-fishing rods.

After moving from one friend's house to another, I spent about half a year living on a campground by a lake. I realized how little we need to live well. I trembled with pleasure at this lightness and freedom I'd never felt before. Finally, I had made my dream come true.

I had devoted most of my time and energy to preparing for this dream. Relationships, career advancement, pride, trends, status … I kept letting them go, one by one, on my path to my dream. My friends asked me, 'Don't you ever feel anxious

EPILOGUE

about letting go of so much?' I couldn't answer those questions then, but now I can say I've never regretted letting go of anything people call 'big'.

People never let go of what they can't live without. Even when you think you've carved everything away, something still remains. The perfect sculpture, hidden within all along, now revealed – your unburdened true self. That is your soul: in my words, your inner artist. Treasure it, and let it guide the journey of your life.

Life is a free journey without a set track and unnecessary rules. Some people carry more baggage for security, while others carry less for freedom. Each has their own life strategy. I chose the life of less – quite radically so. As German architect Ludwig Mies van der Rohe put it, 'Less is more'. Through these experiences, I know this is true.

Don't rush. There's no need to run. Keep walking your own path – nobody else's – at a gentle, steady pace. Don't forget to appreciate the scenery along the way your soul leads you. In Japanese, a path with no set route or goal is called 道 (Dō). Dō is beyond a physical road, it's a spiritual quest for self-refinement. In Dō, pursuing one's own way is the reward itself. It's a philosophy that values the process – the journey – over the goal.

Some twenty years ago, I produced a young singer–songwriter at Warner Music whose debut made history, breaking multiple records. When asked in an interview, 'At eighteen, you've already achieved your dream. What's next?' she answered, 'My dream is simply to keep singing.' She taught me the truth of the *Dō*. Its purpose lies in the walk itself – a journey to reveal and to express your true self. If you can walk as far and as deep as possible, you have truly succeeded. For her, gaining national fame or selling a million records was simply a view along her *Dō*.

Sixteen years have passed since I fulfilled my dream of moving to New Zealand. Now, at fifty-five – once retirement age – I'm still walking my path toward a new dream.

You may remember what I wrote in the introduction – that back in 2019, I let go of my work and income to bet my life on writing my books. Six years later, in 2025, an unbelievable miracle happened. Publishing offers and enquiries about this book arrived from around the world, marking the fifth cycle of the Law of Letting Go in my life.

EPILOGUE

Each time you fulfill a dream, you become freer and get closer to your true self. Until then, that dream was calling you forward, but achieving it releases you and expands your view. Gradually, the next dream reveals itself. It's like backpacking through an endless mountain range. Every time you reach a summit, another majestic one appears, calling you forward. That's how *Dō* – the path of our soul – becomes never-ending. If I hadn't moved to New Zealand, I couldn't have reclaimed my true self. Then I wouldn't have become a writer, and this book would never exist.

My new dream is to meet readers like you somewhere out there on this planet, and help you liberate your true self. Let's walk together towards the beautiful mountain ahead, and even further, staying free and true to ourselves.

This book is built upon my Japanese bestseller first published in 2012, which sparked the minimalist movement in Japan. Later, one editor told me that it is considered one of the earliest books of modern practical minimalism worldwide. In 2024, I released a revised edition, and this English edition was updated and expanded from that version.

LET GO

'Freedom' carries many meanings. Social and political freedom. Freedom of expression, thought and religion. Freedom from unjust arrest. Throughout history, humanity has struggled for true freedom.

The key to life is to keep walking forward, lightly and freely, at your own pace, on your terms. But every now and then, you should rest your feet and sit with me – let's talk as we watch the blessed and radiant morning sun rise.

With love, from the lakeside forest in New Zealand I call home,

Daisuke Yosumi

Afterword

Humanity's Journey to True Freedom – Seven Steps of Letting Go
(Not a history lesson, but a lens for your life)

●

1. After the Hunter-Gatherer Era
(10,000 BCE)
Letting Go of Hunger, Danger and Freedom

Before borders, mankind lived unbounded, with no possessions. The Agricultural Revolution boosted food security and wealth. As populations and surplus grew, power became monopolized and freedom faded.

'For most of human history, we lived freely as nomads, but in constant danger.'

2. The Enlightenment
(seventeenth–eighteenth centuries)
Letting Go of Ignorance

'Mankind is born free; and everywhere he is in chains.'
– Jean-Jacques Rousseau, *The Social Contract* (1762)

3. The Dawn of Modern Freedom
(1789)
Letting Go of Imperial Rule

In the same year, freedom was awakened in France through revolution and in America through the constitution.

'Liberty, Equality, Fraternity.'
– Motto of the French Revolution (1789)

'To secure the Blessings of Liberty to ourselves and our Posterity.'
– Preamble of the US Constitution (1789)

4. The Abolition of Slavery
(nineteenth century)
Letting Go of Ownership

'If slavery is not wrong, nothing is wrong.'
– Abraham Lincoln

5. The Universal Declaration of Human Rights
(1948)
Letting Go of Boundaries

'All human beings are born free and equal in dignity and rights.'
– Preamble of the Declaration

6. Women's, Civil Rights, LGBTQ+, Disability and Indigenous Movements
(twentieth century–present)
Letting Go of Prejudice and Silence

'No one is free until we are all free.'
– Martin Luther King Jr.

7. The Digital Age
(twenty-first century)
Letting Go of Control

'I believe in creating prosperity from technology, ensuring economic fairness, and maintaining personal liberty.'
– Sam Altman

The Ongoing Journey
Gaining True Freedom

'Freedom is not a static gift but a living practice.'